A MENTOR'S COMPANION

REVISED EDITION

LARRY AMBROSE

Photo by Kate McGrath

Larry Ambrose has been an organization development consultant with a special interest in coaching and mentoring for more than 30 years. He, his business partner Jim Perrone and their staff have assisted hundreds of client organizations in making mentoring a key human development strategy. Mr. Ambrose has written *A Mentor's Companion, The Mentoring Field Guide,* and *Common Sense Mentoring.* He has also co-authored *The Mentee's Navigator* with Mr. Perrone. In 2010, Larry turned his attention to producing this Revised Edition of *A Mentor's Companion* to include lessons of experience and mentoring innovations that Perrone-Ambrose Associates has introduced in the intervening twelve years since *A Mentor's Companion* was first published. Mr. Ambrose and his wife Karen live in Chicago.

Corporate Headquarters

Deerfield, IL

800-648-0543

For Karen,
My Life, My Love

Contents

Foreword

In the twelve years since the introduction of *A Mentor's Companion*, my partner Jim Perrone and our staff and I have enjoyed extended engagements of several years with many of our mentoring clients. Those relationships have allowed us to initiate multiple mentoring programs and to witness the results achieved by those mentors and mentees. We have also been privileged to see the outcomes of our efforts and to alter and enrich our approaches to the ever-changing world of mentoring. While techniques of mentoring continue to evolve, the basic principles and truths still apply. Mentoring continues to focus one person's efforts on strategically affecting the professional life of another for the better by fostering insight, identifying needed knowledge and expanding that person's horizons.

This Revised Edition incorporates many of the lessons we have learned over the decade plus since the first edition and contains many new techniques that I hope and trust will make your efforts to expand your mentees' talents and their sense of assurance a success.

I love this quote from Howard Vincent O'Brien:

People work for self-expression
Even when they talk loudest
About "getting the money."
They are really most interested
In doing a job skillfully,
So that others will admire it
And give them that inward glow of satisfaction
Which comes of achievement,
From the painter, producing his masterpieces,
To the truck driver, piloting his leviathan
Across city streets,
The basic thought is:
"I am the best caballero in all Mexico."

I find further inspiration in the words of Max DePree, author of *Leadership is an Art,* "The art of leadership is liberating people to do what is required of them in the most effective and humane way possible." James O'Toole, in his forward to DePree's book, writes, "To do this effectively requires clear thinking on the part of the leader. That is, leaders must be clear about human nature, the role of the organization, the measurement of performance. Because they will have carefully considered such questions in advance, leaders will have the self-confidence, as Max says, to 'encourage contrary opinion' and to 'abandon themselves to the strengths of others.'" In short, the true leader, the true mentor, is a *courageous listener and life-long learner.*

I hope you will carry these inspirations with you as you work with your mentees, searching for ways that you can aid them in becoming their own "best caballero."

I wish to first of all thank Jim Perrone, my business partner and co-learner for nearly 37 years. Every instance of creation and accomplishment by Perrone-Ambrose Associates has been a product of constant collaboration, and thus this book is as much Jim's doing as mine. I want to acknowledge our wonderful clients and the mentors and mentees who have provided us the opportunity to continually discover the evolving nuances of mentoring and coaching. Our staff and consultants have always contributed the "hard questions" that ensured that the creative edge would never be sacrificed. And special thank-yous to Noreen Gorman and Simone Nathan. To Noreen, thanks for your editing and making sure that progress was maintained and that typesetting and printing went off without a hitch. To Simone, my appreciation for your way with words and design and for overseeing the quality of the final manuscript. If not for my good fortune of having all your support on this effort, this Revised Edition would never have been possible.

Larry Ambrose
Deerfield, IL, July 2010

Introduction

Mentoring has always been a vital part of human learning. We have all learned from the more seasoned—our parents, teachers, role models, supervisors, and friends. The word *mentor* itself is as old as Homer; in *The Odyssey*, Mentor is the advisor and guardian of Odysseus's son Telemachus. Mentoring, then, is one person's attempt to guide another. The 1990s brought a renewed and enhanced need for such a personal advisor—especially in corporations. In this book, you are Mentor, and mentoring is your attempt to guide someone through the process of becoming a more fulfilled and productive member of an organization.

Mentors are participating in a kind of revolution. The sheer rapidity of change in business and society has made us question the existence of the corporation as we know it. What threat does downsizing pose to trust in the organization; how do we prepare future leaders in an increasingly complex world; how do we deal with the aging and increasingly diverse work force? These and many other questions cause us to seek guidance about how to respond, how to cope, and how to thrive within a changing environment. Mentoring is not the only answer, but it is a practical response to the need to rebuild the workplace as a locale in which employees can place their trust, realize their potential, and find honor.

But this activity called mentoring has not always been in favor, especially with traditional "command-and-control" type managers. Practices such as coaching, counseling, and listening have often been branded as "soft skills," or part of a "touchy-feely" management style not conducive to the bottom line.

The problem is, the command-and-control leadership style does not produce the kind of employees everyone says they want. Leaders participating in mentoring skill-building programs made a list of employee abilities their organizations are looking for. The list included *taking responsibility, making decisions, solving problems creatively, contributing to the thinking process,* and *supporting the corporate vision.*

If "take-charge" employees are what we want—if we need employees who are creative, courageous, involved, and responsible for their own development—we have to change the tactics we have used in the past. Building a "mentoring culture" is a necessary ingredient for making that vital shift. The mentoring culture mandates that its members help each other not only to produce but to grow; not only to get results but to learn; not only to achieve organizational goals but to become empowered. Mentoring is one of the most powerful developmental strategies known today. In every organization, employees must feel they have the opportunity to learn and grow from the experiences they are having on the job; they also seek some sense of long-term contribution in the workplace.

The mentors of any organization are those who can integrate others into the company. This typically means that the mentors have experience behind them and are willing and able to spend time and effort to develop talent in others. As a part of their mission, mentors give advice, but we're not going to tell you how to give advice in this book. Advice giving comes naturally.

We will concentrate instead on using yourself as a catalyst with your mentee (who we will also refer to as your "protege" or your "partner"). Our mission here is to distinguish and dramatize the skills of the mentor—those probes, those challenges, those inquiries and provocative questions that will inspire thought, stimulate reflection, tap discovery, and generate a new intelligence in your mentee.

Chapter 1 describes the mentoring process, the purpose of mentoring, what it is and what it isn't, and the kinds of skills necessary for you to develop as a mentor. The following chapters will carry you through the mentoring action itself, dramatizing it with examples, guidelines, and specific menus of questions and inputs for interacting with your partner. Each chapter features a different major activity you can expect to engage in with your mentee: *making contact and getting acquainted, working on problems, giving performance and behavioral feedback, making developmental assignments,* and *conducting after-action reviews.* Each of these chapters contains specific guidelines for each meeting with your mentee. These guidelines are summarized on "notepads," like the ones below.

Each chapter also contains more specific guidelines—called Checklists—that are marked with a ✓. You should use these Checklists to prepare mentoring interactions with your partner. They are sometimes generic statements, sometimes fill-in-the-blank questions that you will supply the right word for at the appropriate time. An example for a first meeting might be the

THE MENTOR'S NOTEPAD

➤ *Making Contact*

➤ *Problems*

➤ *Feedback*

➤ *Assignments*

➤ *After-action*

simple question, *"What do you hope to gain from this experience?"* Another example, in a subsequent meeting, might be *"If you could start your project over, how would you do _____ differently?"*

But don't try to plan every part of your mentoring discussion in advance. It's important that you listen closely to your mentee and act appropriately to his or her needs. The checklists only suggest possible topics for discussion, but by reviewing them you can anticipate some of the directions of your meeting and prepare your responses accordingly.

As a mentor, you will build a relationship with your mentee by making contact and getting acquainted. This is explained in Chapter 2, where you will find guides for interviewing your mentee about needs and also find out how best to help. The chapter will also point out ways you and your partner can initiate the mentoring with a clear plan both of you can endorse—one that will serve as a road map for your relationship.

In your role as mentor, you will doubtless find yourself helping your partner as he or she confronts a problem or a crisis. Chapter 3 offers guidance as you attempt to help the person grow and learn from the experience as well as to get the issue addressed.

One of the more challenging jobs for any manager or mentor is giving clear, authentic, and helpful feedback about how the mentee may be holding him or herself back. Chapter 4 contains blueprints and methodologies, not only for becoming more adept at delivering needed feedback to your partner, but for reducing the degree of dread and defensiveness you both might be feeling at feedback time.

Chapter 5 helps you and your partner plan and prepare a project for execution. In Chapter 6, you will work on how to review the project's outcomes with your mentee. Both of these chapters focus not only on the mentoring process but on the project's results. This dual focus maximizes your partner's on-the-job learning and seasoning.

Another feature of this book is a hypothetical mentoring situation between Ruth Merlin, a vice president in a large corporation, and Art Regent, a manager several levels below Ruth on the food chain. Through their conversations and their work experiences, you will be able to see how your mentoring relationship might shape up, from Ruth's and Art's initial meeting through problem solving and feedback.

This is probably not a book you'll want to take to the beach. It's also not a book you will likely read from beginning to end—in fact we encourage you to skip around, using what is most relevant for you at your stage of mentoring. It is, however, a valuable reference and guide for any aspect of the mentoring charge. We hope that you find it to be a highly practical aid as you take on the important challenge of helping others unlock their true potential. That's what it is for. May you realize deep satisfaction—satisfaction you deserve—for accepting the responsibility of being a mentor.

CHAPTER 1

What Mentors Do
(and How They Do It)

"The mentor is both patient teacher and impatient master, encouraging and affirming, then suddenly, challenging a mentee's capacities. At first we wonder what he's doing. Then we marvel at how he seems to know just what to do and when."

—LARRY AMBROSE

Good mentors inspire their mentees to learn and grow; to see new things and new possibilities not only in their jobs, but in themselves. Sometimes the very fact of having a mentor will give individuals confidence enough to move into new areas of experience and make harder decisions involving both themselves and others.

This is your task: to inspire, challenge, and guide your mentees—to instill in them the confidence and responsibility to take informed, calculated risks resulting in a more creative contribution to the job. In the course of your mentoring, you will find that there are several ways to do this. You will be an ally, a catalyst, and a coach. All are important. In fact, you may find yourself switching hats often. Within these three main areas you will find that a mentor must be

- ★ a teacher
- ★ an advisor
- ★ a planner
- ★ a pathfinder
- ★ a protector
- ★ a supporter
- ★ a role model
- ★ a tactician
- ★ a storyteller
- ★ And a lot more.

The Mentor As an Ally

Employees who choose to participate in a mentoring program are serious about their growth and development. That doesn't mean, however, that there might not be some fear or misgivings about what they are getting into and who they are having to deal with.

To give help or to receive it implies trust and a certain openness. For help to be of any benefit, mentees must be willing to be forthcoming about their needs, whether these needs involve knowledge, skill, ability, emotional support, or encouragement. They must be willing to "empty themselves out" in order to let new learning come in. In short, they must feel it is safe to reveal their vulnerability. You can help by opening up a little yourself. Your first job as a mentor is to make them feel comfortable. Let them know that you are on their side. After all, what they really want is to know how you think and how you function on the job. They want to know how you approach problems and what gets your attention.

Trust is the most important part of beginning a mentor/mentee relationship. Without it, there can be little benefit to either party. To have a successful relationship, you both must feel comfortable in expressing your thoughts and feelings. If this can be achieved in your initial meetings, it will be easier to give and respond to feedback later. That implies a partnership in which you are both equal contributors. And as you work closely with your mentee, that initial fear will disappear, replaced by the challenge of learning and growth.

When the mentoring relationship has endured some tests and you both have demonstrated your dedication to it and each other, your dealings will become more natural. A good relationship allows you to show occasional exasperation with each other. Faith in the developing partnership will allow you more freedom to be yourselves. Hopefully, you will find yourself able to be completely spontaneous in your reaction to your partner's progress (or lack of it), worrying less and less how you phrase the feedback. In turn, the mentee will trust that you have his or her best interests at heart and will appreciate your honest and direct response.

The Mentor As a Catalyst

One of the reasons you have taken on a mentoring assignment is that either you or someone in your organization has noticed the potential for growth in your mentee—an interest, an openness, a promise. It is your job to stimulate that promise.

A catalyst is an agent that provokes a reaction that might not otherwise have taken place and, in some cases, speeds it up. One of your jobs as a mentor is to put your mentee into unfamiliar situations and see what takes place. As a result, you will help your mentees become adept at seeing their own responsibility for growth and become farsighted in understanding what they need to do to realize their full potential.

And here's the easy part: the most important thing you can do as a catalyst is to just be yourself. You are a role model that your mentees can look up to and possibly pattern themselves after; the pathfinder whose light points the way through unfamiliar territory. Through your demeanor, reaction to circumstances, style, work habits, strength, passion, and compassion, you are a role model for the kind of person the partner can aspire to be. Best yet, role modeling is all the more inspiring if you are also the *vehicle* by which the mentee can achieve those aspirations. This means that, in addition to being an object of emulation, you become an active agent, energetically helping your mentees to realize their full potential. One way to achieve this is by sharing some of your wisdom and experience. In this way you will be accelerating their growth by giving them something that they would otherwise have had to learn the hard way. At other times you may decide that the best way for your mentees to learn is to put them in the battle and have them duke it out for themselves. That's when you become the real *agent provocateur*—the one who stands in the center of a situation of your own making and monitors what goes on.

So how do you decide when to shine a light or when to light a fuse? That's where strategy comes in.

It is said that Dean Smith, head basketball coach at North Carolina, was such a consummate coach that if you asked him, "When do you think the sun will rise tomorrow?" he would answer, "Why are you asking that? Where are you going with that question? What do *you* think?"

Some answers are easily given, others are not. When they are not, you may have to coach your mentees through the learning experience much like a basketball coach draws up a game plan. To do this you will have to become both a strategist and tactician.

As a strategist, you will assist the mentee in selecting and organizing experiences for growth and learning. Specifically, you and your mentee must discuss the person's long-term developmental goals, consider work assignments or experiences aimed at fulfilling those aims, and track progress. Such assignments may involve exposing your mentee to particularly challenging experiences that he or she might not encounter if not for your involvement. These assignments can be challenges such as fix-it projects, start-up programs, joint tasks with another department, or coaching a less experienced individual—whatever you think is appropriate. It is important that you make use of these real-life situations as teaching opportunities.

In the tactical sense you will be helping the mentees grow and learn from their experiences, whether planned or serendipitous. The coaching you do on these occasions—which may be either prior to or following an assignment or experience—should have the effect of drawing out the mentees through listening and questioning, tactics which will test their thinking and propel them to analyze steps of action and consider alternatives. In this capacity, you try to empower the mentees to think critically, make choices, and commit to a thought-out course of action. In doing this you are expressing your conviction and confidence in your mentees' intelligence and ability.

It is important, even crucial, to cultivate and nurture a trusting and sustaining mentor/mentee relationship—one in which you and your mentee will have a great affinity for one another. But if you ignore or do not develop the tactical communication skills of coaching, you will inevitably fall back on giving advice, telling stories, and providing your mentees too many answers that they would be better off producing for themselves. The mentor who is equipped with tactical mentoring skills eventually succeeds in "growing" the mentees to the empowered position of being able to solve their own problems and make their own decisions. And that is one of the ultimate goals of mentoring in the first place.

Your aim is to be "generative;" that is, to produce new development, to seek excellence, to help the mentees surpass themselves. In doing this, you will be using two important skills: listening and asking questions. These two essential skills are much more easily discussed than practiced. We'll discuss them briefly below; the remainder of the book will be devoted to their practice.

The Mentor As the Driver

Mentoring is about the mentee. The emphasis of both your efforts and those of your mentee should be on identifying, clarifying, and pursuing your mentee's developmental goals. You may need to emphasize to your mentees that they have an agenda in mind for their mentoring, that it is essential that they know what they want from it and are open to growth and change. Some mentees may think that you know better than they what will most benefit them. Our work with mentors and mentees over the years has provided us with incontrovertible proof that this cannot possibly be true. The mentee must develop goals, sometimes with your help, and be willing to pursue them. The mentee's job is to let you know what they want and need and then to pursue it with purpose and energy. You should expect this and let them know that you expect it. You may work together to jointly compose your mentees' agendas, but the direction must be driven by the mentee. Your mentees must be the drivers in the relationship. They must give the relationship its energy by making demands on it and on you. If you have a mentee with no agenda, you do not actually have a mentee. A mentor cannot mentor without a mentee.

Ensuring that your mentees take the driver's seat is the first step in empowering them to greater strength. You have many different roles as a mentor. But all of your roles—catalyst, strategist, guide, teacher, coach, etc. must have one guiding mission – to make your mentees stronger, more able to confront situations successfully, and to own their commitment to growth and learning. Anything you can do that makes your mentees stronger, you should begin or continue doing. Anything you do that makes them more dependent on you, you should avoid or discontinue.

Level 2 Listening

Chances are, if you are thinking about mentoring someone you are an accomplished problem-solver. The most common obstacle that many great problem-solvers encounter in trying to be mentors is that they want to solve problems! It's what you do best. It's what you feel comfortable doing. If a mentee presents you with an issue on which he or she needs mentoring, there is a strong, almost irresistible, tendency for you to take over and give advice—to solve the problem. When this happens, you are a victim of traditional thinking about the helping process. You view the act of giving help as "doing for" the mentee. You have been seduced by the problem, and you respond by taking over the thinking from the mentee. Here, you are mentoring the problem instead of the person. This is the point at which you should ask yourself, "What is my agenda? What should I be doing as a mentor right now? Is it to help my mentee grow? Or is my job to get the issue resolved?"

True mentoring is aimed at the mentee's development—not on solving specific problems. When specific problems or issues are addressed in a mentoring context, they are most fittingly used to contribute to long-term learning and application by the mentee. The "fixing" of a problem may well be appropriate in a given situation, but the real mentor is always interested in the larger lessons that can be derived from solving it. So what do you do when your mentee has a problem and asks for help? Do you

★ tell a story?
★ give advice?
★ give the answer?
★ provide a framework for discussing the issue?

There are no hard and fast rules about what you should do from a tactical point of view, except one: *listen*. Listen for what the mentee needs, what he or she is looking for, what the *real, true, underlying issue* is. There are two levels of listening: Level 1- Internal Listening, and Level 2- Focused Listening.

When you are listening at Level 1, you are listening literally. This means you are listening for the words, the problem, tangible information. At Level 1 you are also listening to internal chatter in your head, your own ego needs, for an opportunity to provide any answer to your mentee.

People, especially mentees, send signals by every means—words, body language, facial expressions, super subtle body and facial messages. These bits of information are coming a mile-a-minute, and guess what, you are picking them up, maybe unconsciously—through your ears, eyes, and even your gut, your "whole body satellite dish". But if your attention wanes, is interrupted or divided, your satellite dish gets disconnected and you fall back on your own thoughts and preconceptions.

When you listen at Level 2, your focus is totally on your mentee. You are listening for what the person is saying *beneath the words*. You are listening for the underlying issues, needs, and feelings. You are listening for expressions, emotions, what's important to the mentee, what is not being said. You hear the uncertainty in the voice as well as the confidence, and what gives the person energy and what makes him or her withdraw.

By listening at Level 2 you will be able to figure out the most appropriate form of help to offer. If you listen only at Level 1, you will likely misunderstand what the true issue is. And if you fail to see what is really going on, you will either misdiagnose the direction in which to go or you will give answers and advice that are not as relevant as they should be.

Level 2 Listening means, literally, to listen in order to understand—but not sympathize with—where the person is coming from, what he or she is feeling, thinking, or experiencing. It's not that you should be unfeeling, far from it. It's just that you have an active responsibility to understand both the *content* and the *emotion* involved in the message. In short, you will be trying to "read" the message the mentee is really sending, whether he or she is actually *saying* it or not.

You get two things from listening at Level 2. First, you get a highly confident definition of the true issue or problem and what the underlying causes

might be. If you are going to bother to mentor on an issue, you'd much rather be working on the *right one*—the real issue—than wasting time on symptoms.

Second, you get what is called a "contract"—recognition by your mentees that you truly are listening to what they are saying, that you understand where they are coming from, and that their issues are important to you.

Listening at Level 2 allows you to articulate what you're hearing, clarify your understanding, pinpoint the underlying issue, and invite the person to be innovative and creative in exploring himself in relation to the situation.

When you achieve Level 2 listening, it is almost always apparent to the other person. He or she can sense when you are attuned to what they are thinking and feeling. The result of this connection is a growth in trust and a willingness to be more open in the relationship, making it more possible to communicate authentically and provide assistance more on the mark with the person's actual needs.

Through Level 2 Listening you focus on the mentee, on how that mentee is approaching the issue, and on what he or she is willing to commit to. You can then assist in the thought process, not taking over but allowing the mentee to be influential in shaping the outcome. By empowering the mentees to think and confront what the real issue is, they will be able to "do for themselves" instead of being dependent on you.

Level 2 Listening leads to the other helping skills of the true mentor. These skills are characterized by the questioning process.

Asking High-Gain Questions

One of the most powerful ways to mentor the person as well as the problem is the creative use of the probing or questioning process. And because of the tendency toward becoming a "doing for" helper, mentors often find it incredibly difficult to simply *ask questions.* When mentoring, it is seductive to suddenly feel that the best way to help is to offer answers, suggestions, and recommendations. Asking high-gain questions—questions that seek more than a "yes" or a "no" answer—puts you in the tactical mentoring role.

Disciplining yourself to ask questions before jumping in with ready answers dramatically changes the mentee's experience.

There are as many reasons to ask high-gain questions as there are mentors and mentees, but here's a list of the most important.

★ It ensures two-way communication in the mentoring relationship.
★ It helps the mentee think through issues instead of having you do it all.
★ It reduces the mentee's defensiveness toward whatever suggestions and ideas you choose to offer.
★ It discloses your mentees' thoughts on issues, giving you a greater opportunity to help them clarify courses of action to which they can commit.

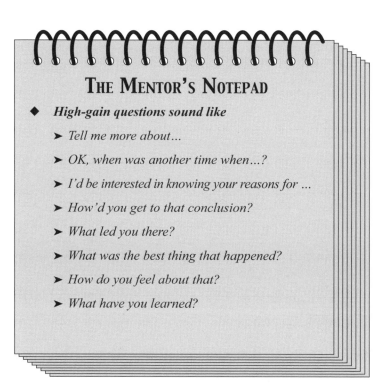

THE MENTOR'S NOTEPAD

◆ *High-gain questions sound like*

➤ *Tell me more about...*

➤ *OK, when was another time when...?*

➤ *I'd be interested in knowing your reasons for ...*

➤ *How'd you get to that conclusion?*

➤ *What led you there?*

➤ *What was the best thing that happened?*

➤ *How do you feel about that?*

➤ *What have you learned?*

High-gain questions are of three distinct types and fulfill very different objectives. They are *investigative, discovery,* and *empowering.*

Investigative Questions

When discussing issues with a mentee or when reviewing the events of a project or an assignment, it is common to simply seek information. Before you can even decide on what kind of help to offer, you need background information on the event. You need information on the history of a project, its personnel, its difficulties, its importance, and so on. The high-gain questions you will ask in this pursuit are called *Investigative Questions.* Investigative questions seek information, objective data, and facts—usually from the past in order to understand the present. Investigative Questions sound familiar because they are the ones we most commonly ask. They are the "what," "when," "who," "why," and "where" questions.

While important, investigative questions are a limited and preliminary part of the mentor's tactical business. Investigative questions usually benefit the mentor more than the mentee. Because they cover familiar ground and deal mostly in facts, the mentee can usually answer them quickly and impersonally. They are low-risk questions that result in low gain and limited learning for the mentee.

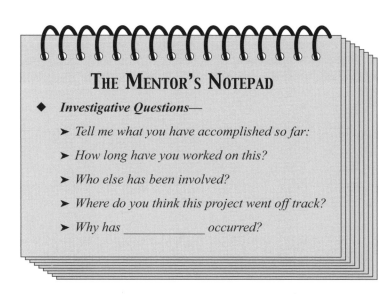

THE MENTOR'S NOTEPAD

◆ *Investigative Questions—*

➤ *Tell me what you have accomplished so far:*

➤ *How long have you worked on this?*

➤ *Who else has been involved?*

➤ *Where do you think this project went off track?*

➤ *Why has _____ occurred?*

Discovery Questions

Obviously, investigative questions are not enough. If you want to examine the mentees' reasoning and stimulate original thinking, you're going to have to ask questions that dig deeper into their own knowledge and experiences. These are called *discovery questions*, and yield high-gain responses. They are intriguing questions that prod the mentee into exploring conclusions and learning from experience, into gaining new knowledge or insight from things they already know.

Discovery Questions are *not* familiar, because we don't think to ask them very often, if at all.

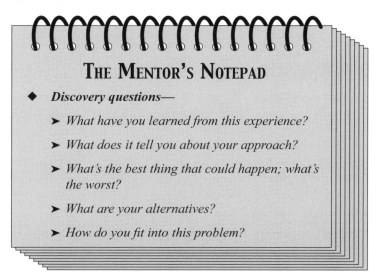

THE MENTOR'S NOTEPAD

◆ *Discovery questions—*

➤ *What have you learned from this experience?*

➤ *What does it tell you about your approach?*

➤ *What's the best thing that could happen; what's the worst?*

➤ *What are your alternatives?*

➤ *How do you fit into this problem?*

These are the "you" questions—questions that focus on the other person. They always include a provocation to think and to make an interpretation. They will give you an idea of how much risk mentees are willing to take in certain on-the-job situations.

If your mentees are to take ownership of the actions that result from your mentoring, deeper, more subtle questions are necessary. These are the "payoff" questions that transfer ownership for action to the mentee; they are the *empowering questions.* Empowering questions push for action. They inquire directly into what your mentees are ready for, what they want from an action, what their plans are, and what they are ready to commit to.

These questions will help you turn the corner from information and awareness to action and results.

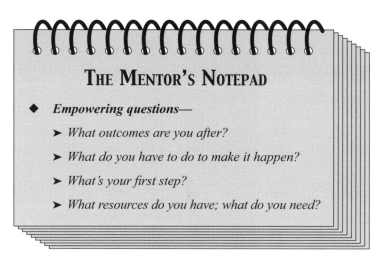

THE MENTOR'S NOTEPAD

◆ *Empowering questions—*

➤ *What outcomes are you after?*

➤ *What do you have to do to make it happen?*

➤ *What's your first step?*

➤ *What resources do you have; what do you need?*

Your Internal Checklist

At this point you may be asking, "How do I decide how to mix these questions; how do I decide which questions to ask and when to ask them?" We said at the beginning of this chapter that what the mentee really wants is to know how you think. You must realize that you are a seasoned individual who has evolved your own way of thinking. You have an "internal checklist" that you rely on to guide you in your decisions. One of the most valuable things you can teach the mentee is how to access your internal checklist. This is infinitely more valuable than teaching the person the answers to various questions and problems. By verbalizing your various checklists for thinking, you will be providing your mentees with important problem-solving and decision-making equipment that they can use to determine their own moves in the future. In doing this you are guiding the development of their critical thinking.

When you use the high-gain questioning process, you are, in essence, using your checklist out loud. By asking questions strategically, you are operating by your checklist. By asking questions of your mentees, you are not only asking them to answer the questions, you are simultaneously transmitting your checklist to them. You are taking the mentee through it step by step. This does not mean that you will script out your questions in advance. Just be aware that you have a checklist and use it actively in the dialogue. Let your mentees know that they should be learning your checklist. Because they are interested in how you think, learning your internal checklist lets them find not only the answer but the route by which *you* would have arrived at that answer.

But be careful here. Being a seasoned, experienced individual presents you with a fundamental problem. The very definition of seasoning means that your actions and responses to issues have become imbedded in you; you may perform them as naturally as breathing. They are what you do. Therefore, when you are confronted by a mentee with a need or a problem, you may have to reach deep inside to access your imbedded checklist. The effort and force necessary to retrieve it may result in its coming out in the form of a quick answer (taking over the thinking from the mentee) or in an impatient judgment expressed in surprise or exasperation that the mentee does not know something that is so obvious to you. So be on your guard and be prepared to reshape your ready rejoinder into a listening and probing response.

Thoughtful and creative use of these high-gain questions is indispensable for energizing the mentee through the thinking, planning, and execution process so key to his or her growth and development.

CHAPTER 2

Making Contact

"The lightning spark of thought, generated or, say rather, heaven kindled, in the solitary mind, awakens its express likeness in another mind, in a thousand other minds, and all blaze up together in combined fire."

—THOMAS CARLYLE

SCENARIO 1

Ruth and Art

Ruth Merlin is a highly respected manager at Signal Satellite Communications. An engineer and MBA, she has been at Signal for fifteen years, and in that time has risen five levels—from staff engineer to her present level of vice president of the Cable Division. At 47, her responsibilities include overseeing four remote facilities and 627 employees, and most people agree that she is destined for even bigger things.

Entering her well-appointed office, you are aware of walking into the realm of a very busy executive. Progress charts and graphs are strewn in a seeming haphazard fashion around her conference table; mounds of papers and open project books are piled up on her desk and bookshelves. Her wall calendar with its innumerable notations and changes denotes an informal, results-oriented leader. Pictures of her husband, children, and extended family occupy less cluttered areas of her desk and and walls and provide one quiet note to the busy office.

Ruth is interested in success, but she is also motivated by a desire to give something back. As she has succeeded in the company, her experience, maturity, and personal growth have created a desire to pass on what she can to others and over the last few years she has become a successful teacher. In fact, her division has become something of a "farm system" and recruiting grounds for future executives. Budding managers vie for an opportunity to work for Ruth.

This year Ruth volunteered to be a mentor in the company's Management Mentoring Initiative (MMI).

Art Regent is the 33-year-old manager of the Insulation Division at Signal. He, too, has a degree in engineering, but little experience in administration. The fact that he has reached his position without such experience says a lot about his skill as an engineer and his self-motivation. Art enjoys the demands of managing; however, he realizes that his lack of experience may hold him back if a promotion comes available. Hearing about the MMI—and about Ruth Merlin's involvement—Art was quick to sign up. Bob Armis, Art's supervisor in the Insulation Division spoke with both Ruth and Art approved Art's participation in the project.

As Art entered Ruth's office for their get-acquainted or "linking-up" meeting, Ruth got up from her desk, shook hands, and motioned him over to the conference table.

"Just move some of those papers and sit down," she said. "I told my secretary to hold my calls, so we won't be interrupted for a while." She sat down across from Art and smiled at him over a sheaf of graphs.

"I keep meaning to clean this place up but I never seem to have the time."

"Looks like my desk," Art replied.

Ruth laughed. "I'm not sure that's a good thing or not," she said.

"But at least it gives us something in common. Now tell me why you're here."

Art looked confused. "I thought…"

Ruth came to his rescue. "I mean why did you sign up for this program? What do you think about this mentoring thing? What do you think you'll get from it?"

Art looked down and fingered one of the graphs. "I'm not sure I can put it into words," he said. "But when I heard about it I told myself that it was something that I couldn't not try for. I've never had what I'd call a mentor, so I don't have much of an idea about what to do or what it could be for me, but I wanted a chance to work with you if I could.

"What kind of help do you think I could give you?"

He looked up. "That's hard to answer, really. I guess… well, I'd like to see how you attack things. I'd like to know how you think."

"So you're not going to be looking for answers?"

"Well, yeah, sometimes, but you've been pretty successful. Like, how'd you get that way, you know? What do you look for in solving problems, things like that."

"All right, so far so good. I've never been anyone's formal mentor, either, so let me ask you a few questions. First, what are your short-term goals—like six months or a year out?"

"Well, the first thing that comes to mind is promotion and the extra responsibility that goes with it. That's one of my goals—to make Project Manager and get to Engineer 3 level."

"How about the money that goes with it?" Ruth smiled.

"That, too."

"And what to you think will help you get there?" Ruth asked.

"Well, exposure to as much design and project management as I can get."

"You're a little iffy on how to do both at the same time?"

Art nodded. "That's it exactly."

"I think I could help with that," Ruth said. "I had to learn the same thing, sometimes with more stress than I would have liked."

Art brightened. "I'll tell you what I'd really like—to head a complete system fabrication project.

"Maybe I can help with that, too. What would you say comes easiest to you?"

Art smiled. "That's easy. The engineering part. Working out the problems, designing solutions. I'm on that like white on rice."

"And what's the biggest challenge? The toughest stretch?"

Art's expression became more serious. "That's easy, too. The managing and the people stuff. I don't consider myself inept at it, but you asked about the toughest stretch. Trying to motivate people who don't see—or maybe don't want to see—the problem and solution as clearly as I want them to is a push for me."

"Handling people is a challenge for all of us," said Ruth, nodding. "So what would you say your main goals are for the mentoring experience? No, wait, that sounds too formal. How do you see our working together?"

"Well, right now, I think they are pretty much what we've talked about. I'd like you to help me learn how to balance it all—maybe learn how *you* do it. I'd like to be able to ask you questions if I get in a bind. One thing I really need is to be able to come to you when I need some advice, or need to think something through. Maybe you could help me think about it different-ly. Does that make sense?"

"Sounds pretty reasonable," nodded Ruth. "But I'm getting the idea that you want me to be available on an as-needed basis. What do you see as *your* responsibil-ity in making this work?"

"Well, I didn't really mean that. I think my responsibility includes letting you know when I want or need something, but I know how busy you are. My need may not correspond neatly with your availability. But do we have to set up formal meetings every time I have something I want to run by you?"

"No, of course not. If I'm not able to respond to you immediately, I'm sure we could talk within a reasonable time. As I think about it, it may be a good idea to have a kind of schedule, like a set time each month to check in, so we don't lose track of ourselves. My guess is that we won't be dealing too often with emergencies. That kind of thing is probably between you and Bob Armis."

"Right, I would think so."

"All right, Art, I think you understand what your responsibility is—and what mine is." Ruth was all business now. "I expect you to take the work we do very seriously and to be open to my ideas and feedback. I'd like you to be open to trying new ways of doings things and I want you to be be willing to experiment with pushing yourself fairly hard sometimes. I expect to

ask you to try some things that may be a lit-tle scary, but they are things that helped me in the past. How about checking in, oh, say, the third Thursday of the month?"

"Um, all right, sure."

"I hope I can bring something of value to the table. In any case, I'm prepared to listen to you and try to respond as effec-tively as possible. I have a few ideas and suggestions that I'll give you as we move along, and as we get to know each other better, we'll both be able to come up with the things that will benefit you most. Now, let's work on some specifics."

Art gulped. "Now?" he asked.

"Sure, why not. I've talked with Bob, and I want you to go with me to a man-ager's meeting on Friday.

"You mean *this* Friday?"

"You have another appointment?"

"No, no. I can be there."

"It'll be a good opportunity for you to see how a few things are done. They don't expect me to bring anyone, but I've decided you should come anyway. So here's the deal; you sit in the corner and say nothing. You are wallpaper. Listen to what everyone in the meeting says and, without taking notes, notice what they are *really* saying. Then I want you to sit down with me on Monday and summarize what you heard and what each manager really *communicated*."

"You think I'm ready for that?" he asked.

"If you weren't," she told him, "you wouldn't be here."

Making Contact

You and your mentee need to formally meet to set up your relationship. You should bring your preliminary plans to this "linking-up" meeting and be ready to discuss your views thoroughly with each other. The link-up gives both of you the opportunity to learn each other's ideas, needs, and goals for the mentorship, and to find out what you each expect from the mentoring process.

Both you and your mentee must contribute to developing a good mentor/mentee relationship. Your partner should see the mentoring as a key career opportunity; you should view it as a chance to influence your mentee's growth and as a chance to learn and broaden yourself as a leader. It is your joint responsibility to develop a relationship in which you can share real trust. If you don't trust each other, the mentoring will not be successful.

This relationship-building process begins the first time you and your potential partner get together. In this link-up meeting, you are initiating the "sizing-up operation," looking each other over. You both should approach the link-up with open minds, but with some clear objectives.

Although you are both responsible for the success of the meeting, it is the mentor—you—that is accountable for making sure your discussion produces clear results, even if those results are that you agree *not* to proceed. In a way, the dialogue resembles an interview, at least in the early stages.

A Few General Guidelines

Ask your mentees about their strengths and weaknesses. What do they need to work on? What are their strong points? How do they see their opportunities for growth within the organization?

Find out your mentees' short-term and long-term goals. Everyone has hopes for the future. Find out your mentees' aspirations and career goals. This knowledge will guide you in constructing relevant developmental goals and in managing your mentoring with a mind toward their fulfillment.

Let your mentees know what you want and need from the relationship. If you don't get anything out of the experience, the partnership can't be expected to survive. In fact, it won't be a real partnership at all.

Have a frank and honest discussion of your expectations of each other as mentor and partner. It is important for each of you to give this serious thought *before* the meeting so that you can state clearly what you need from each other in the relationship and how you will know if the mentoring is delivering what you both are looking for.

Agree on clear and reasonable objectives for the mentoring. This will include such diverse items as formalizing developmental goals for the mentee, constructing coaching and training plans, and working out ways to evaluate the ongoing progress of the mentoring itself.

Decide the logistics of your partnership. How often will you conduct formal meetings with each other? Which of you will be responsible for ensur-

ing ongoing informal communications? How much access will the mentee have to you?

As the mentor, you have primary responsibility for kicking off and leading the link-up procedure. If you do it well, you will have created a strong base for an open and responsible partnership. Through it, your mentees can begin to exert joint leadership and shoulder the ultimate responsibility for their own future development.

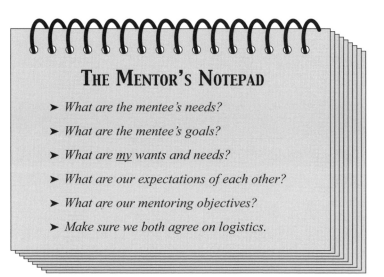

THE MENTOR'S NOTEPAD

➤ *What are the mentee's needs?*

➤ *What are the mentee's goals?*

➤ *What are my wants and needs?*

➤ *What are our expectations of each other?*

➤ *What are our mentoring objectives?*

➤ *Make sure we both agree on logistics.*

Always Begin with Some Questions

The getting-acquainted and trust-building process is most often made easier by asking good interview questions. When you can exchange answers to probing questions of real interest to both of you, you and your mentee get a great chance to learn about each other and solidify your impressions.

Of course, mentors don't just ask questions. The link-up is a critical get-acquainted activity, and the mentee needs to know about you, too. This is the time to let the partner know what you are looking for and how you perceive the mentorship. Make sure you establish some ground rules about how you should communicate and how candid and frank the mentoring relationship should be if it is to work.

A good mentoring relationship starts with preparation by both parties. It is even a good idea for you and your partner to develop a written "contract" for how you intend to work together. This agreement would include:

★ specific short-term and longer-term objectives of the mentorship
★ preliminary developmental goals for your partner

- ★ what you both want to get from the mentorship
- ★ what you can each contribute to it
- ★ how often you intend to meet formally
- ★ how you will handle informal contacts and meetings between formal sessions
- ★ which of you has the chief responsibility for driving the relationship
- ★ the degree of candor you hope to encourage in each other
- ★ when your first planned session will be scheduled
- ★ any needs for confidentiality
- ★ your role as mentor versus the role of the mentee's manager

Your Lessons of Experience

It is important that you become as aware as possible of what you have to contribute and how your potential contributions can match the needs of those you are mentoring. The mentees, too, might prepare a list of questions about what they hope to get out of the mentoring relationship.

The Checklists on the following pages will give you an idea of the use of probing questions and other issues you will benefit from clarifying.

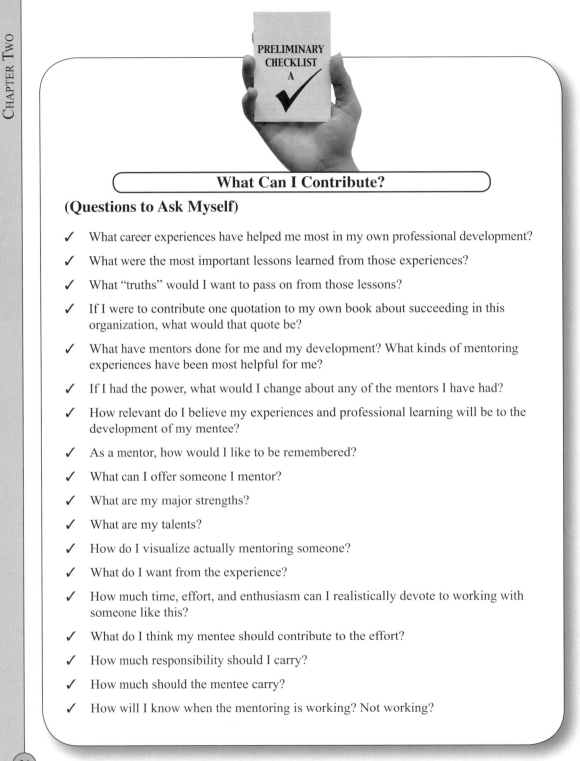

PRELIMINARY
CHECKLIST
A
✓

What Can I Contribute?

(Questions to Ask Myself)

✓ What career experiences have helped me most in my own professional development?

✓ What were the most important lessons learned from those experiences?

✓ What "truths" would I want to pass on from those lessons?

✓ If I were to contribute one quotation to my own book about succeeding in this organization, what would that quote be?

✓ What have mentors done for me and my development? What kinds of mentoring experiences have been most helpful for me?

✓ If I had the power, what would I change about any of the mentors I have had?

✓ How relevant do I believe my experiences and professional learning will be to the development of my mentee?

✓ As a mentor, how would I like to be remembered?

✓ What can I offer someone I mentor?

✓ What are my major strengths?

✓ What are my talents?

✓ How do I visualize actually mentoring someone?

✓ What do I want from the experience?

✓ How much time, effort, and enthusiasm can I realistically devote to working with someone like this?

✓ What do I think my mentee should contribute to the effort?

✓ How much responsibility should I carry?

✓ How much should the mentee carry?

✓ How will I know when the mentoring is working? Not working?

PRELIMINARY
CHECKLIST
B

What the Mentee Wants from the Mentoring

(Questions Mentees Should Ask Themselves)

✓ Do I want a mentor?

✓ What do I think a mentor should do for me?

✓ What are my strengths?

✓ What are my major needs?

✓ What would I like to know from a mentor?

✓ If I had a mentor, what are the most important things that person could help me with?

✓ What are my short-term job objectives?

✓ What are my long-term career goals?

✓ What do I expect to contribute the mentoring process?

✓ What do I bring to the table?

✓ What should my mentor do for me?

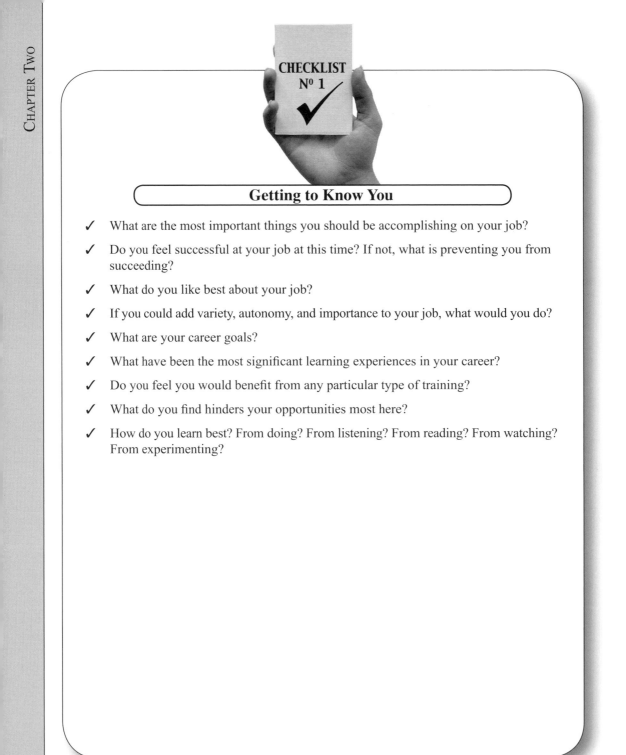

Getting to Know You

✓ What are the most important things you should be accomplishing on your job?

✓ Do you feel successful at your job at this time? If not, what is preventing you from succeeding?

✓ What do you like best about your job?

✓ If you could add variety, autonomy, and importance to your job, what would you do?

✓ What are your career goals?

✓ What have been the most significant learning experiences in your career?

✓ Do you feel you would benefit from any particular type of training?

✓ What do you find hinders your opportunities most here?

✓ How do you learn best? From doing? From listening? From reading? From watching? From experimenting?

**CHECKLIST
Nº 2**

What Would Benefit the Mentee Most?

✓ What knowledge, skills and abilities do you feel I possess that would most benefit you?

✓ What kinds of special learning or improvement opportunities do you feel I could provide or help you get?

✓ What do you want to know from me?

✓ What do you want most from me?

✓ What information do you have for me on how I can best help you or better understand what you need?

✓ What are you ready to bring to making this mentorship work?

✓ What do you need right now?

✓ What is the best way to give you feedback?

✓ What scares you?

✓ What makes you want to learn more?

✓ What do you feel you lack talent for? What is the toughest stretch for you?

✓ What is your most satisfying success?

✓ What is your most disappointing failure?

What Do I Want from the Mentoring

✓ What are your goals for this mentorship?

✓ What do I offer that most interests you?

✓ How can you get it in the most beneficial way?

✓ Are you seeking

- advice?

- training?

- apprenticing?

- brainstorming?

- experience?

- a sounding board?

- coaching?

- shadowing?

- an example?

- history?

- assignments?

- exposure?

- an advocate?

- strategy help?

- political connections?

- pathfinding?

- a working partnership?

- something else?

**CHECKLIST
Nº 4**

What Do I Bring to the Party?

✓ How will you know when it is not working?

✓ Describe the degree of frankness you seek in our dealings. Be specific. Give me examples.

✓ How will you know when you have what you're looking for?

✓ What are your responsibilities in this mentorship as you see them?

✓ What are mine?

CHECKLIST
Nº 5

Other Issues to Discuss with Mentees

✓   This is the skill or knowledge I can offer.

✓   This is my hope for what I can bring.

✓   This is how I see myself as a mentor.

✓   This is what I expect to devote to it and to you.

✓   This is the time I can give.

✓   This is what I would like to expect from you.

✓   This is how I'd like to relate to your manager.

✓   This is how often I think we could meet.

✓   This is how I'll know when we're in trouble.

✓   This is how I'd like our communication to be.

✓   This is how much initiative I'd like you to take.

CHAPTER 3

Mentoring in a Problem Situation

"An expert is one who knows just that much more about the subject than his associates. Most of us are nearer to the top than we think. We fail to realize how easy it is, how necessary it is to learn that fraction more."

—WILLIAM N. HUTCHIN

SCENARIO 2

Ruth and Art

It is a Thursday afternoon following Ruth and Art's initial linking-up meeting and they are sitting at Ruth's conference table again. This time the charts are stacked in neater piles and pushed to the other end of the table. Her desk, too, is more orderly, with fewer books and papers to see over. After nearly a full day of work, Ruth is still relaxed while Art seems more disheveled than usual. His greeting is polite, but cursory, and he keeps glancing at his Blackberry.

"I'm glad to see you, too," Ruth began. "I was planning to talk about the meeting last Friday, but you look like you have something else on your mind."

"It shows?"

"It just looks like you're having one of those days."

"Well, I'll jump right in, then. Two of my people aren't getting along and I need a sounding board about what to do about it. Usually, I'd go to Bob with this kind of problem, but I think it's time to learn how to handle something like this myself. And if I can solve it without his being involved, so much the better."

"I'm listening," said Ruth.

"One of my project managers is having a personality conflict with a technician on his shift—just doesn't seem to be able to deal with him at all."

"And why is this a problem?" asked Ruth.

"Isn't it obvious?"

"Is it?"

Art sat back with a puzzled expression. "Well, both of them have come to talk to me about the other." Art scrolled down the screen of his Blackberry, rolled his eyes and put it back on the conference table.

Then Ruth asked, "What's your role in this? What do you want to accomplish?"

"I want it solved, but in a win-win for everybody. I'm just not sure it can be done." He held up the ball of paper. "I tried to make some notes about the situation, but couldn't come up with anything useful."

"You're pretty concerned about this," Ruth said.

"Yeah, I'm really uncomfortable about it."

"Is this conflict affecting the project?"

"Yes, in two ways—tasking and delivery. The project supervisor isn't getting what he needs. Vital communications are breaking down. The whole thing could seize up and I'll have to take over and save it."

"Just like you've had to do before?" Ruth asked.

"Right."

"I understand where you're coming from," Ruth nodded. "Well, let's look at it more closely. What's the problem between them? Why can't they get along?"

"The technician is very independent, very strong willed…"

"Stubborn?" smiled Ruth.

Art nodded. "Exactly. He doesn't take direction well— sometimes, not at all."

"So it's the technician's manageability and the supervisor's inability to deal with him. If the technician suddenly gets easier to manage, will the problem go away?"

"Absolutely," said Art quickly, then he added, "But I don't expect that to happen."

"Who's looking for you to do what?"

"I'm responsible for the scope of control on the project.

Bob knows that something is going on, but not exactly what. I'm not—the project is not—going to succeed if this continues. We need to make adjustments of some kind…"

"Whoa," said Ruth. "Slow down a little. You've been too close

to the problem for too long. Let's talk about Friday's meeting for a while, then go back to your problem later."

"All right. Maybe I do need a break from thinking about it."

"Let's jump right in then," said Ruth. "What did you see Charlie doing in the meeting?"

"Charlie? He strikes me as a very creative guy with lots of ideas. His market forecasting of the insulator business really took the big picture into account. I was wondering if I could ever think that expansively. But he seemed to gloss over a lot of your questions—especially about some of the dangers we might run into in the future."

"So?" Ruth asked

"I'd feel a little uncomfortable letting a guy like that make a decision that might get us into trouble come crunch time."

"What was his *real* message? What was he really after?"

"I think that was it. He really felt his forecast was good and wanted to sell it."

"I don't think so," Ruth countered. "Yes, he was trying to sell his untested idea, but all he seemed really concerned about was winning. I don't think he's as committed to his proposal as he is to being seen as influential and important."

"Wow. I missed that part. Would I have seen that if I knew him better?"

"Maybe. But you should train your ear and your eye to watch for subtle indications of a person's true motives. I watch Charlie like a hawk, and I test him hard on every one of his ideas. How about Louise? What did you see there?"

Art looked at the ceiling. "She's so quiet, it makes her hard to read. She didn't say much at all, but when she did, it seemed to be very appropriate and related closely to what had been discussed. She was very nice and cooperative in the meeting." Art thought for a moment. "But she was taking no risks. I still don't know what *her* opinions are; she's keeping them hidden. I'd like to know what she's really thinking."

"I agree. So what do you think her standing in the group is?"

"It's got to be fairly low. She doesn't add much to the thinking process—maybe because she's afraid of being wrong. And that's too bad because she seems to be quite bright."

Ruth was impressed. "You got her right. I've talked to her many times about this, how she gives up power and influence by being so worried about being wrong. It's interesting that you saw it that clearly, coming in from the outside. It will give me another angle for mentoring her on it, that it shows so obviously. Thank you. Tell me about Greg."

"This guy is almost scary, especially when he gave his report about the late delivery of those smart pallets to Storage Unit 4."

"Why was that scary?" asked Ruth. "Wasn't his report detailed enough?"

"Way *too* detailed. All that stuff about inaccurate technical specifications and weigh-bills and you name it. I couldn't figure out what the hell he was talking about. Then I noticed something: all the time he was talking, he looked at everybody in the room except one."

"Pauline Blackshear?"

"You noticed?"

Ruth smiled. "I think you've hit it pretty accurately. So tell me what was really going on?"

"I don't think the report was really about the pallets at all. I think that Greg and Paula just don't get along and instead of dealing with it, they just have these little skirmishes in the meetings."

"Good ear. But does that sound familiar?"

"You're talking about *my* problem, now, right?"

"Um hmm. So far you've told me about the project manager's

problem and the tech's problem, but what's the *main* problem?

Who's not confronting what?"

Art hesitated, glanced at the notebook on the table, then at Ruth. "I guess what I'm really afraid of is having to deal with it at all."

"Bingo," smiled Ruth.

"I need guidance on approaching the personality conflict myself."

"So," she said, "can we put aside the project issues for now?"

Art nodded.

"O.K., how does the personality conflict manifest itself?"

"Well," Art answered, "It's like I said before. The guy—the technician—is very difficult to manage. He's totally not a team player. He whines and won't cooperate."

"Why not just give him his walking papers?"

"He's too valuable to the project—very advanced technically. We can't do without him. Ditto for the supervisor; his other projects have been excellent."

"So," Ruth said, "what do you want for an outcome?"

"I want them both working together," Art answered. "And I want them working toward the project end. I want them on the same sheet of music."

"Tell me what you've done to deal with this. Have you talked to them about their responsibility to get along?"

"Not exactly," Art admitted.

"Why not? What's stopping you?"

"I don't exactly know. I thought it might make it worse,"

"Sounds like you're not comfortable bringing it out in the open," Ruth told him. "What's scaring you?"

"I don't think I'm scared exactly. I'm just not sure what I'd do if it got complicated—if I really confronted one or both of them."

"If you *did* confront them, how would you do it?" she asked.

"Well, one thing I've thought about doing is sitting down with each of them and getting their take on the situation. Getting each one's input on their own solutions to it."

Ruth nodded. "Good. How do you think that would go down with each of them? Especially the technician?"

"O.K, think. Yeah."

"Anything else you'd do?"

"Then I might bring them together so we could discuss ideas for a solution."

"Do you think it'll be that easy?"

"I think it will be a very hard meeting."

Ruth sat back and folded her hands on her lap. "Here's what I'm thinking right now," she said. "I know this technician. What would happen if you just straight-out told him how his behavior is disrupting the project and demand that he wake up to it?"

"Boy. Maybe that's what I need to do, but …"

"I'm not insisting. But let's try working on that a little. What would he say if you just told him straight?"

"I think he would be flabbergasted. I don't think he has any idea how he's perceived. Or maybe he does but just doesn't care."

She offered, "Maybe he does care. Ever think of that?"

"Umm. I've never thought about him that way. You think maybe he's just trying to make sure that he gets heard?"

"What do you think?"

"It's possible, I suppose …"

"Okay, then. How are you feeling about talking to him in this way now?"

"I think I can do it," Art told her firmly.

"All right," Ruth replied. "So what's your plan?"

Art thought for a few seconds, then said, "The first thing I'm going to do is to talk to the project supervisor and find out how things stand as of right now. Then, depending on what he tells me, I'll deal with the technician. I'll tell him he's the monkey wrench in the works. Then I'll see about bringing all three of us together."

"So far so good," Ruth told him. "Now let's brainstorm how you'll approach this "honesty" meeting with the technician. How will you begin; what'll you say first?"

Solving Problems—Not Giving Away Too Many Answers

We've been trained all our lives to come up with solutions. We've been told that when someone asks for help we should *help them*. We have instilled in us the impulse that when anyone—cousin, sister, or mentee—asks for help we give them the benefit of our wisdom and experience. The temptation to take over, give advice, tell the person what to do, or at least what *we* would do in a like circumstance is close to overwhelming. To be sure, people often seek advice, and sometimes advice is exactly what is needed. But not always.

As a mentor, your job is to help your partners to grow and develop their own problem-solving abilities. That objective often demands that you *not* give advice; that you not even answer every question you are asked. It demands, instead, that your mentees be pushed to examine the issues and their own motives. Because the stated "problem" is not always the real problem, you must take real care not to be seduced into coaching the "problem" only. The puzzle here is that we all have been trained to sniff out and solve *problems*. Your charge as a mentor is to *coach the person as well as the issue,* because the person's "problem with the problem" is often as big an issue as the original problem itself. This is where Level Two Listening really comes in; you must not let your problem-solving zeal interfere with listening for the *real* issue and how your partners are feeling about it. They may be frightened of confronting the problem, or frustrated and angry with another individual involved without knowing how to handle it. Mere expert advice may provide the "right answer" and still not deal with their reticence or personal inability to confront the situation and take action to solve it.

Your job here is to probe and listen to how your mentees are viewing and reacting to the issue at hand. You can then use investigative and discovery questions to help them examine their own thinking process and get clarity on what the real problem or issue really is. Once the real issue is out on the table, problem-solving can at last begin. Then you can assist your partners through further questioning—and maybe a little advice—to develop a decision on an effective course of action. This is an excellent chance for you to use the listening and questioning process to take your mentees through your own internal checklist for examining problems, as we discussed in the first chapter.

While you do not wish to dictate your partner's decision on a course of action, your mentor's role demands that you ensure that the dialogue proceed in a conscious way toward a clear conclusion.

A Few General Guidelines

You must help your mentee to identify the true issue, not just symptoms, so that irrelevancies can be discarded on the way to an effective outcome. You have to be constantly concerned with helping your partners organize their thinking and problem-solving. This often means digging down to issue identification, which leads to discovery and action.

Once you have helped identify the real issue at hand, your job also includes investigating the causes of the problem or situation and listening closely to how your mentee feels about the issue. At this point, empathetic listening is essential in sizing up the importance of the issue and shedding relevant light on possible actions to resolve it.

Your mentee may be part of the problem, either through faulty judgment or by choosing not to confront the situation. It is important that you stay alert to this possibility and be ready to question your partner on it; indeed, he or she may be the *real* problem!

In your capacity as mentor, you are not only interested in getting the issue resolved; you must be just as attentive to the learning value of the process. Remember to push your mentee to examine his or her own thinking about the issue and to analyze in a critical manner the various alternatives and consequences attached to it.

When you feel that your partner has thoroughly assessed the issue and owns responsibility for it, push for action. Ask empowering questions, such as

- ★ "What do you want as an outcome?"
- ★ "What must you do to make it happen?"
- ★ "What are your obstacles?"
- ★ "What's your first step, and when are you going to take it?

Keep these steps in mind, not as a formula, but as a mental model to ensure that you always help your mentee to clarify his or her own thinking in preparation for reaching a decision and committing to a course of action.

Questions and Answers

As you try to aid your mentee's thinking process, it is appropriate and important that you use the high-gain questioning process extensively—but not exclusively. Your mentees wants to know what you think about the issue, their approach to it, and what suggestions you have for resolving it. You are not being helpful when you deny them your thoughts and opinions. That is refusing to share your wisdom and your experience about what works and what doesn't. So you must find a way to mix your input of suggestions, opinion, and your position on the issue with questioning and listening in a way that results in your mentees coming out with a decision they can own. It is essential that you give them ample opportunities to develop their own thoughts and ideas before you begin your shower of suggestions. If you give in to the temptation to roll out your propositions before letting your mentees generate thoughts and proposals, you will tend to dominate, and the resolution of the issue will likely belong more to you than to the individual. Contribute your knowledge and experience but only to what the mentees need, not what *you need to give them*. With that caution sign erected, below are some categories of suggestion to consider when mentoring on a problem or a specific issue. You can probably think of many more.

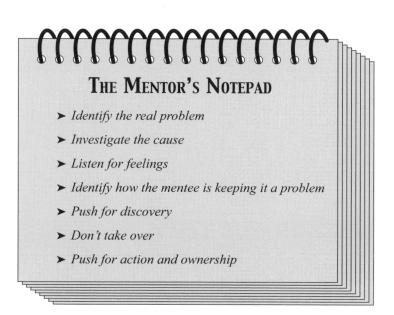

THE MENTOR'S NOTEPAD

➤ *Identify the real problem*

➤ *Investigate the cause*

➤ *Listen for feelings*

➤ *Identify how the mentee is keeping it a problem*

➤ *Push for discovery*

➤ *Don't take over*

➤ *Push for action and ownership*

Empowering Your Mentee

  It is so easy for a mentor to dis-empower a mentee. All you need to do is forget about listening or about asking questions, and "help" your mentee by offering solutions to every issue brought up or problem experienced. Many mentors have management, leadership or technical expertise. One set of habits is apropos for these responsibilities; quite a different set of competencies is relevant to mentoring. As you acclimate yourself to the role of mentor, you will find that it is often more effective, even if you know how to resolve your mentee's issue, to resist offering solutions and facilitate the person's ability to analyze the issue, consider alternatives, create solutions and develop commitment to carry through with appropriate actions. If you must make a choice between getting the issue resolved or the ensuring that the mentee learns and becomes stronger, the mentor must choose the latter. Your mentoring success or failure is not defined in terms of how many issues you resolve. It is defined by how strong, resourceful and self-sufficient the mentee becomes.

  The Mentor's Compass is a guide for the mentor in empowering the mentee. It is provided to aid you in managing yourself in your mentor/ mentee communication and resisting the temptation we all feel to become the *problem-solver* instead of the mentor. The guidelines offered in the Compass are presented in a wheel arrangement to indicate that empowerment is not a linear, step-by-step process but a fluid interaction in which you intentionally consider the appropriate action to fit the needs of the mentee.

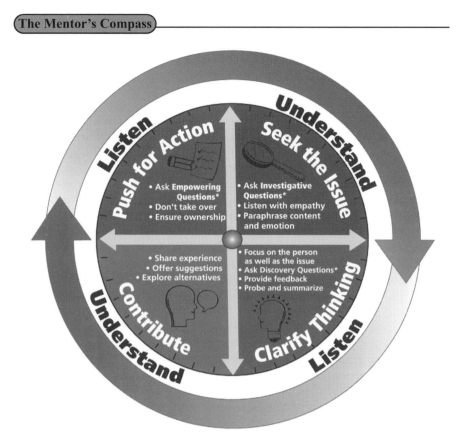

Although the Compass is a non-linear guide, it is important to pay attention to two of the steps as you begin your interaction with your mentee. Always begin with **Listen** in order to **Understand,** and never lose your emphasis on listening deeply to your mentee. The entire mentoring function depends on the mentor's ability to listen and understand. The diagram indicates that listening does not occur in only a one-time manner; it must be ongoing if the mentoring is to be successful.

Next, **Seek the Real Issue**. Effective listening is essential if you are to identify and understand the mentee's real issue. The mentor should always be vigilant in searching for the true issue or problem that is facing the mentee, and must probe for the feelings behind it. This may take some time and effort, but it is essential if you are to be effective in addressing what is relevant to the mentee.

Clarify Thinking. The mentor is actively concerned with helping the mentee think as critically as possible, through probing into his or her reasons and intentions. Helping clarify a person's thoughts and feelings on an issue

is key to aiding him or her to develop a plan for making a clear decision and developing the commitment to resolve his or her issue.

Contribute. Mentoring is more than listening and asking questions. The mentee also needs the opinions, knowledge and other input from the mentor. The mentor often possesses experience the mentee does not. Suggestions, advice and perspective are often invaluable in gaining a direction. The mentor, however, must guard against taking over and solving the issue for the person. Helping is not "doing for." Real help enables the person to do for him/herself.

The goal of most mentoring encounters is to move the mentee to take some action, so **Push for Action** is often the concluding step in the mentoring conversation. Action is not always the desired outcome of mentoring, but the mentor always asks him/herself, "Is this a situation that calls for an action? If so, what can I do that will enable the mentee to get up and do what needs to be done?"

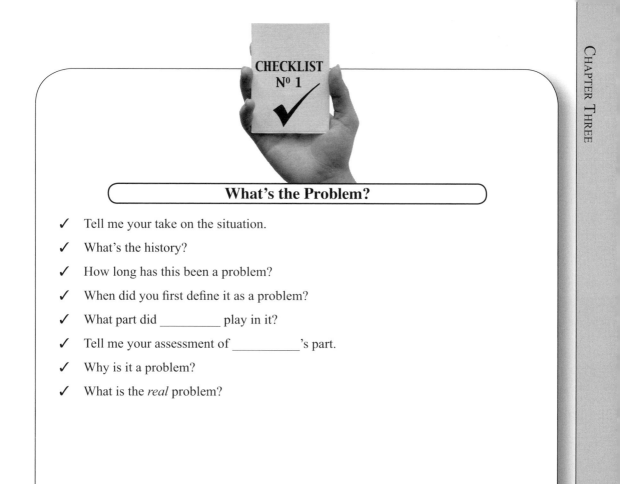

What's the Problem?

- ✓ Tell me your take on the situation.
- ✓ What's the history?
- ✓ How long has this been a problem?
- ✓ When did you first define it as a problem?
- ✓ What part did _____ play in it?
- ✓ Tell me your assessment of _____'s part.
- ✓ Why is it a problem?
- ✓ What is the *real* problem?

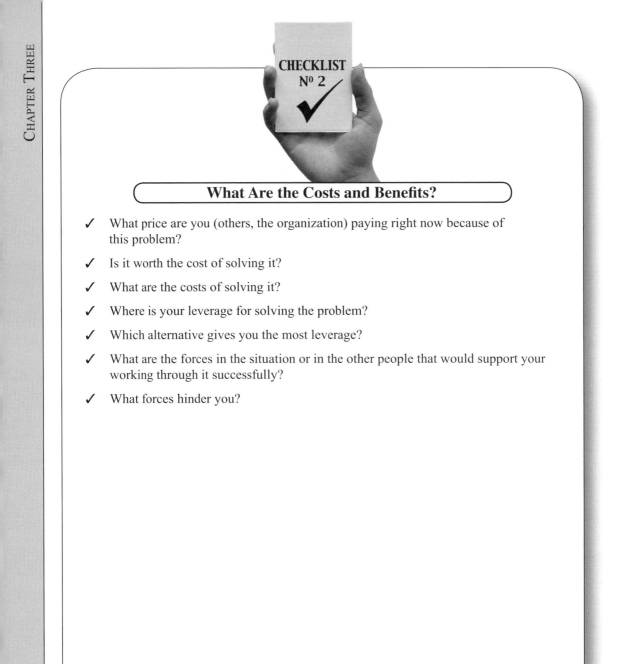

What Are the Costs and Benefits?

✓ What price are you (others, the organization) paying right now because of this problem?

✓ Is it worth the cost of solving it?

✓ What are the costs of solving it?

✓ Where is your leverage for solving the problem?

✓ Which alternative gives you the most leverage?

✓ What are the forces in the situation or in the other people that would support your working through it successfully?

✓ What forces hinder you?

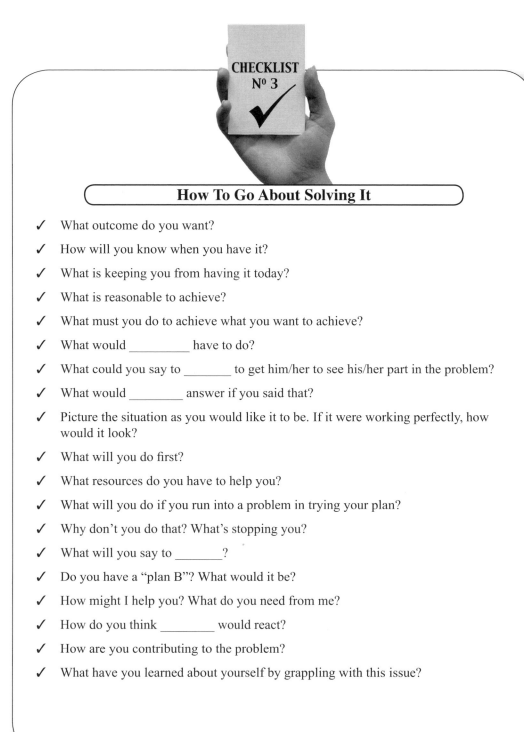

CHECKLIST Nº 3

How To Go About Solving It

✓ What outcome do you want?

✓ How will you know when you have it?

✓ What is keeping you from having it today?

✓ What is reasonable to achieve?

✓ What must you do to achieve what you want to achieve?

✓ What would _____ have to do?

✓ What could you say to _____ to get him/her to see his/her part in the problem?

✓ What would _____ answer if you said that?

✓ Picture the situation as you would like it to be. If it were working perfectly, how would it look?

✓ What will you do first?

✓ What resources do you have to help you?

✓ What will you do if you run into a problem in trying your plan?

✓ Why don't you do that? What's stopping you?

✓ What will you say to _____?

✓ Do you have a "plan B"? What would it be?

✓ How might I help you? What do you need from me?

✓ How do you think _____ would react?

✓ How are you contributing to the problem?

✓ What have you learned about yourself by grappling with this issue?

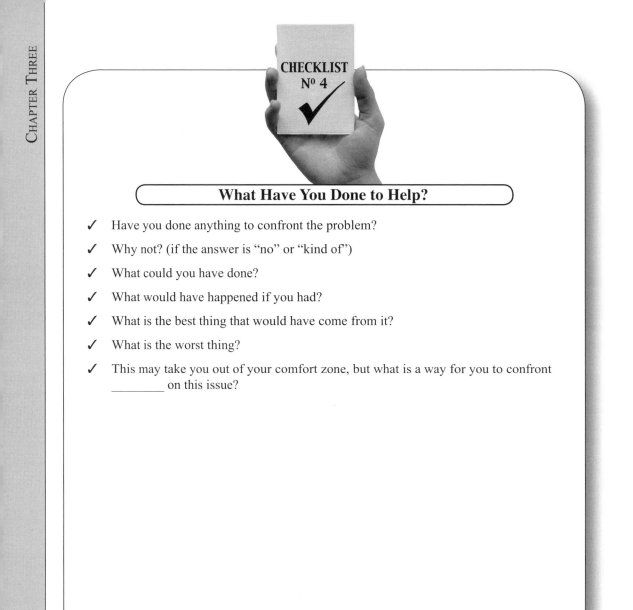

What Have You Done to Help?

✓ Have you done anything to confront the problem?

✓ Why not? (if the answer is "no" or "kind of")

✓ What could you have done?

✓ What would have happened if you had?

✓ What is the best thing that would have come from it?

✓ What is the worst thing?

✓ This may take you out of your comfort zone, but what is a way for you to confront _____ on this issue?

CHECKLIST Nº 5

Suggestions

✓ This is what I could envision the possibilities to be.

✓ How about _____? He/she might be of real help.

✓ I agree with that approach.

✓ What if you did this in addition to that?

✓ What if you did what you're suggesting, but position it in this (a different) way?

✓ What would happen if you did this _____?

✓ This is the way I have approached it in the past.

✓ Why are you suggesting that? Do you believe that will work best?

✓ What would be the best thing that would result from that?

✓ I think what you're suggesting will run into this _____ difficulty, because _____.

✓ I think you will need to achieve this _____ end; this is the real bottom line.

✓ Tell me how you would disagree with that; bargain with me.

✓ We need to get there by _____. How will you do it?

CHAPTER 4

Giving Feedback

"Not everything faced can be changed, but nothing can be changed until it is faced."

—JAMES BALDWIN

SCENARIO 3

Ruth and Art

Ruth is having Art work with her on planning and executing a cable system emplacement project for one of her major customers. The purpose of Art's involvement in the project is for him to use it as a mentoring experience with Ruth. The project has advanced through the planning stage, and implementation has begun. They have been meeting with the customer's operations manager and staging of the project is about to begin.

Ruth has been observing Art closely in these meetings. She feels it is time to give him some of her reactions. She has asked Art to review his most recent work with the operations manager and get together with her that afternoon.

Overall, Ruth has been rather pleased with most of Art's dealings with this manager. But there were some issues she felt that Art should become aware of, both for his own growth and for the outcome of the project. He had been having some problems understanding what the customer really wanted, and at times would get so focused on what seemed right to him that he would forget to check in with the operations manager in the proper way and at the appropriate time. On top of that, when he would become aware of this tendency, he would overreact and agree to incorporate everything the customer asked for, regard-less of the wisdom of doing so.

Ruth began the meeting, which took place in her office as before.

"Have you done some internal review of how your dealings have been going?" she asked.

"Yeah, I've been going over the last week piece by piece."

"Good," she said. "What did your review tell you?"

Art sat back and put his hands behind his head. "Well, it's interesting what you dig up when you really stop and look at what you've been doing. Overall, I think it's not going too badly. I haven't been involved with a project like this before—at least all the way from planning through emplacement. The thing I came up with most is that I think I'm too agreeable when they make a demand."

"I agree, Ruth said. "Why do you think that happens?"

"I'm not sure. I know how *I* think the system should be put in and when I get a project fixed in my head I usually go for it. At the same time I know this is an important customer with ideas of his own."

"So? Give me some more analysis."

"Maybe I'm just trying too hard to please him and am afraid of making him mad by disagreeing with him on something he obviously wants."

"Is that really it? Or is it something else?"

"It sounds like you have an opinion on this," Art said.

"Yes, I do," Ruth acknowledged.

"Well, before you tell me what it is, let me say one more thing. I don't think I lack backbone; as a matter of fact, I'm almost too set in my ways, but I'm not sure how to handle difference of opinion diplomatically. I'm seeing that if they leave me alone, or I don't give them a chance to disagree, I have no trouble just going with something I think is right. It's when they start making suggestions…"

"Okay, stop right there," said Ruth. "I think you see what I'm getting at. Number one, I see you not soliciting the operations manager's input. You're so focused on the task that sometimes you don't see anything else. But sometimes you act almost as if you don't *want* input."

"No," Art began. "I *do* want input." He stopped, then began again. "I shouldn't think I know everything there is to know about … I mean, I could benefit from outside help, but…"

"But what?"

"It'll slow things down. It might take them in a direction I'm not anticipating."

"Maybe so," Ruth said. "But what's more important? The inconvenience of slow-down and change or getting the best thinking on the project?"

"Obviously, the excellence of the outcome."

"Absolutely—and I think the project will turn out well. But what about this tendency to agree with everything the ops manager asks for? I think that's as big an issue as you not getting input in the first place. When you agree too easily your own valuable ideas have less weight. I saw you do that yesterday when he asked you to alter your routing plans. It really seemed odd to me. I knew you didn't agree with him, but you just stood there and let him push you around. That could be dangerous. If he gets the idea that he can get what he wants every time, he may start asking himself if he really needs you on the project at all. It's a double edged sword."

"Maybe I'm a little hesitant because it's really my first time   doing this and I don't want to screw it up."

"He doesn't know that," Ruth reminded him.

"That's true, but that routing thing was such a small point that I didn't think it was worthwhile arguing with him."

"And if it were something bigger, like going with a different brand of transmitter or trying to get around using the local utilities company for our receivers?"

"I see your point. I've been thinking like an idiot."

"You've just been behaving unconsciously, and sometimes when we become aware of that we start to wonder about our intelligence. But it's necessary to see it for what it is and how it effects what we do. Then look into doing something with it. Remember the problem you had with the technician a couple of months ago? You're dealing with almost the same thing here."

Art nodded. "You mean my confidence in dealing with people."

"That's right," she said. "And after a little negotiation that project came out fine. But here you're not dealing with someone working under you."

"Right," Art agreed. He thought for a few seconds, then said,

"In this case I need to be sure enough of myself that I can listen to suggestions from someone who knows the project as well as I do without having to either completely give in or become completely defensive."

"I couldn't have put it better if I had all day," said Ruth.

"But how do I do that?" Art asked.

"Oh, I have plenty of ideas," Ruth said. "But I want to know what *you* think."

"Well, I think I'm technically prepared, but not socially, if that makes any sense. I need to approach a project with the realization that the client might have some last minute ideas. Maybe I can even anticipate some of these ideas and be ready with a response. I don't really want to beg anyone for last-minute ideas because they might think I don't have the situation in hand, but maybe if I ask them for feedback at certain stages, they'll feel more involved in the decisions."

Ruth asked, "Do you think that will help you deal with the ops manager a little differently now?"

Art looked more confident as he said, "I think it will."

"In what way?"

"Well, just what I said before. I probably need to make a list of the things I should ask him for his suggestions on. And be sure to ask him early, before I begin to take the ball and run with my ideas."

"That way you won't have as much to feel defensive about."

"Yes, and I think that will do away with a lot of the suggestions that have been coming late in the process. When the suggestions have been a surprise I just haven't had the right response handy—like I haven't had the ammunition I needed to push back."

"OK," Ruth said, "but it's not always going to happen the way you want it to. Some inputs and suggestions *will* come later in the process."

"I know. I know. I'll just have to keep my head, recognize it, and deal with it."

"Okay, so far so good. But tell me how you'll be able to keep your head."

"Hmm. I don't know. If I could do that we wouldn't be talking."

"How are you going to take responsibility? Nobody's gonna do it for you. How can you manage yourself on this?"

There was a long pause before Art finally replied, "Would cues help? Maybe I could work up some cues to remind myself that when I'm about to fold, don't be afraid to respond with appropriate arguments. Something like that."

"Tell me how I can help," Ruth said.

"You've helped me already by getting me in touch with this," he said. "But I can think of one more thing that might help. Maybe you could remind me occasionally. If you see me forgetting to use my cues, help me to stay aware of my tendency. Better yet, if you see me doing it, either stop me or grab me soon afterwards and let me know that you saw me doing it again."

"I can do that," Ruth smiled. "But enough of the project. Tell me about this discussion. Has it been any help?"

Developmental Feedback

A big part of a mentor's job is giving feedback on what you have observed in your mentees. In fact, they are depending on your honest impression of them and your clear, helpful reaction to what you see in them. You are one of their major sources of learning, a pathfinder whose take on their headway and patterns of conduct serves as a beacon of guidance for furthering their growth and progress.

Providing such honest feedback can be a challenge; it's not something many people are comfortable doing. But you are in a position to be completely honest and open with your mentees. You are not responsible for their performance; you are responsible for helping them learn from their experiences and from your reactions to them. Therefore, you have no axe to grind, no narrow performance objective and as such, you can be the perfect person to "hold up a mirror" to your mentees and let them see what you see.

The manner in which you approach the feedback situation will in large part determine how your feedback will be received. Your goal is to try to make the experience as growth oriented as possible for both you and the mentee. You will find that you will most often provide mentees with "developmental feedback." Developmental feedback is concerned mainly with helping mentees to become aware of patterns of behavior or communication they are unaware of that may be hindering them. Developmental feedback is not directly connected to the acceptable quality of work the mentees are doing; it is aimed at equipping them with awareness of what they can do to surpass themselves.

The Developmental Mindset

It is essential that you always have a developmental intent when giving your impressions to mentees. So when you give feedback you must be committed to having a "Learning" versus a "Blaming" conversation. Blaming is about judging and looking backward, learning is about understanding and looking forward. Unlike performance feedback from one's manager, the mentee's acceptance of developmental feedback is discretionary at the mentee's option. So what mentees think about your intent will affect how they think about you and your feedback.

Feedback conversations are almost never about getting the facts right; they are about different perceptions, interpretations and awareness. They are also an opportunity to get alignment of such issues by the mentor and mentee. You must consider that the mentee may see a situation through a very different lens than you. When you give these principles your clear attention, your ultimate commitment to the mentee's success and well being will be communicated and will make all the difference.

7-Steps for Giving Unsolicited Developmental Feedback

1.   Ask permission to give the feedback.

2.   Acknowledge one of the person's strengths, qualities or goals and cite an example.

3.   Identify what gets in the way of expressing the strength/quality/goal (it can be a behavior, a style issue or, the strength in overuse).

4.   Ask for the person's response.

5.   Ask: "What do you want to do about this?"

6.   Ask permission to give your suggestion(s).

7.   Ask: "What are your next steps?" and "How can I support you?"

Some General Guidelines

Be specific in your praise and in your true impressions of the mentee's achievements, and describe the effect the person's outcomes are having on the job and on others. When you are absolutely clear and descriptive in what you like and do not like in your partner's performance or behavior, the person gets a real picture of what you expect and any differences between what you are expecting and what he or she is delivering. People who know what you want have at least a chance of fulfilling your expectations. If you are not explicit, your mentee can only surmise, or guess, what is essential to you.

Emphasize learning. The real reason for feedback is to help learning to occur. Corrective feedback should be given when someone's performance needs to be amended or when mistakes have been made. The saying goes, "Those who don't make mistakes don't make much of anything." You should welcome mistakes by your mentees as great learning opportunities. Each mistake provides you with another great chance to add to the education of your partner by simply asking, "What did that experience teach you?"

Discuss possible alternative courses of action with your mentee. Summarizing what your mentees have learned from their experiences—especially from their mistakes—opens up the opportunity for talking about contrasting ways of getting the job done. Viewing feedback in this way allows you to consider every incident of giving feedback as an opportunity to enrich the quality of learning.

Offer your help. The classic review process "How did it go?, What have you learned?, and How can I help?" not only enables you to discuss a person's performance and what has been learned, it helps to plan effective next steps. Feedback is help. And it should result in authentic assistance for your partner to become more effective and successful.

Here are some additional reminders to guide you through the feedback process.

★ Sharing your impression of someone's behavior or performance is never—*and should never be*—risk-free.

★ You must be able to state your views truthfully and in no uncertain terms.

★ The mentees will not have been helped if, after the feedback session is over, they still don't know how you actually feel about their outcomes and behavior.

★ You must own-up to what you are thinking and find helpful ways of presenting it.

THE MENTOR'S NOTEPAD

➤ *Hear self-assessment*

➤ *Name impressions*

➤ *Specific praise and correction*

➤ *Tell the effects*

➤ *Use mistakes for learning*

➤ *Ask what is being learned*

➤ *Analyze the alternatives*

➤ *How can I help?*

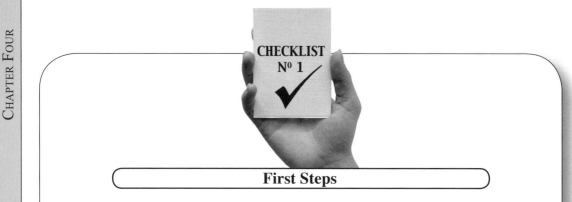

First Steps

✓   Ask the person to do an assessment:

- I want you to do an assessment of this (task) (project) (performance issue)

- I'd like to discuss it to see what we can both learn from it.

- Share your assessment with me. How did you do on this?

- What would you say worked out best? (agree or disagree and discuss)

- What worked least well? (agree or disagree and discuss)

CHECKLIST Nº 2

Here's My Feedback

✓ Here's my (praise or criticism) as I see the performance

✓ This is my picture of what good performance on this will be.

✓ This is how I would like to see it done.

✓ This is what I want.

✓ This is how soon it should be accomplished.

✓ This is the price we'll pay for not making it.

✓ This is the help I can give you (or get for you).

✓ I need an early warning system. How will you provide that?

✓ This is how satisfied/unsatisfied I am.

Exploring Your Feedback

✓ How does this feedback jibe with your own perception?

✓ Tell me your interpretation of my feedback to you.

✓ What do you feel are my expectations?

✓ How do you think the job will look when I am satisfied?

✓ What further clarification do you need?

**CHECKLIST
Nº 4**

✔

What Are You Learning?

✓ What would have happened if _____?

✓ What would have been a better outcome?

✓ What help did you need? What help did you solicit?

✓ When did you first see that you needed help?

✓ What kept you from getting the help you needed?

✓ What have you learned from having this problem?

✓ What other factors led to the problems you encountered?

CHECKLIST
Nº 5

What Can You Learn from Here?

✓ If you could plan this all over, what would be your plan?

✓ If you could do the thing all over, what would you do?

✓ How would you do _____ differently?

✓ How would you ask for help if you could do it all over again?

**CHECKLIST
Nº 6**
✔

What Happens Now?

✓ What are your expectations of yourself next time out?

✓ How will you make it happen?

✓ What do you need in terms of time, resources, follow-up?

✓ How will you keep me informed of progress or problems?

✓ What will you do?

✓ What are you learning from what went well?

✓ How do your successes compare with your problems? How are they different?

✓ What does this teach you?

✓ When are you ready to start?

✓ What alternative methods would you use?

✓ What do you agree with in my feedback?

✓ What do you disagree with?

✓ Overall, how do you feel about the feedback?

CHAPTER 5

Making a Developmental Assignment

"Character is formed, not by laws, commands, and decrees, but by quiet influence, unconscious suggestion and personal guidance."

—MARION L. BURTON

SCENARIO 4

Ruth and Art

Ruth was largely pleased with Art's progress. He had worked through his problem with the operations manager for the cable emplacement project and as a result the project had gone off well. Now it was time to prepare a report on that project and present it to the top brass at Signal. Ruth thought that Art could benefit greatly by participating in both the report and the presentation. She would do part of the presentation, aided by her manager of cable customer liaison, Janine Baker. But she thought that Art could take on the major portion of the show.

Ruth talked her idea over with Bob Armis, Art's supervisor. She wanted to get Bob's take on the idea and to make sure this assignment would not intrude significantly on Art's regular job duties.

"Well, Ruth, to tell the truth, Art's plate is getting full. I don't know if I could spare him for that much work outside the department." he said. "I don't want to hamper your mentoring, though. What do you have in mind?"

"I think that Art needs a little more self-confidence in dealing with people—especially influential people. He's been doing okay so far, but sometimes it's been difficult for him. A challenge like this could kick him into another gear altogether."

"He needs to feel a little more upper management stress, you mean," Bob laughed. "Listen, Ruth. I've talked to Art about this before. He's a talented and intelligent engineer. He's ultra-confident about what he can do personally, but tends to quake in his boots when he has to deal with power people."

"He hasn't had much opportunity to do this before, has he?"

"Not much," Bob agreed.

"Won't it scare the hell out of him?" Ruth smiled.

"Ha! You bet it will. And it's interesting that we just so happen to be in the midst of a project of that order right now. Art has been involved enough to be able to take on an important role in the final report."

"Well, if you're offering a real challenge for him that would be more valuable than something in my shop."

"But could you possibly spare the time to observe and give him feedback on something like this?" asked Bob.

"The role of "outside mentor" might be even more valuable for Art than what I was considering… and not all that time consuming for me, either. Let's do it. But I'll need a little briefing."

That afternoon she phoned Art to set a time when they could get together. Later that afternoon, they met in Art's office in Building E. Ruth had been in Art's office several times before, but only briefly. She remembered it as a small but very tidy place—a niche for everything and everything in it's niche. So she was a little surprised when she walked in and found Art on his knees on the floor sifting through a sheaf of charts that were too large for his desk. He looked up when she entered and got to his feet quickly. He removed some papers from his visitor's chair and piled them on the edge of his desk.

"Hey, Ruth," he said. "Have a seat."

"Those are ceramics tension analyses, aren't they?" she asked.

"Yeah, and there's some charts on the wall, too. It's been a good experience, but it's like I have it on the brain." Art sat down at his desk and straightened his tie."

"When Bob and I talked he said you could really use the experience of reporting results to upper management and that you had been doing a very good job on your part of this project."

"Did he really?"

Ruth added, "He said you really know your stuff."

"Hey, I knew that was the case all along," Art laughed. "But it would be nice if he mentioned that to me. Maybe he could use a little mentoring on that."

Ruth sat back in her chair. "So what do you think happens now?"

"Well… I write a report? I hate that stuff. Uh oh, you wouldn't be smiling like that if you didn't have something in mind."

Ruth responded, "Right."

"I knew it."

"You're going to get a lot out of this," she told him.

"Uh-oh, is this going to hurt you more than it does me, or vice versa?"

"Neither, I hope. Seriously, the best way to learn from a project like the ceramics tension analysis is to see it through to the end. You want to see the benefits and consequences of your work, and the best way to do that is to write it out. What I want you to do is to write up a report of the project, then prepare a presentation for the top management committee."

"Who's going to present it?"

"You."

"Whoa. Should I be honored, or scared?"

"I hope a little of both. Bob said you did a good job on the project and I think you can do a good job on the report."

"Okay. So what's involved?"

"Process and outcomes," she said. "What you did and how you did it."

"Summarizing, organizing, writing, Power Point?"

"That and whatever else you need."

"When does it need to be ready?"

Ruth paused. "The report by the 25th and the presentation by the 30th; that's almost a month."

"Do you think it can be done in that length of time?" he asked.

"It has to be," she said. "What kind of approach do you think you'll use?"

Art looked worried. "I'm not even sure where to begin," he said.

"Okay, that's a pretty easy one. What does every report need to start with?"

"Well, an introduction, I guess."

"And how does an introduction begin?"

"I think I'd start with the purpose and goals of the project in the first place."

"Absolutely," agreed Ruth. "Then what?"

Art was concentrating more easily

now, scribbling notes on the back of an old memo. "Then I'd want to talk about how the actual product compared to the plans. I guess I'd want to finish up by presenting the overall outcomes and contrasting them to the original goals, taking in all the glitches and obstacles we confronted."

"I'd also suggest you cover the *intermediate* objectives and how you planned to achieve them. And be sure to explain any deviations and the reasons for them. I'm warning you right now, you're going to want to know these things to be able to really assess the quality of the project."

"I see. I can do that. I know all that stuff in my bones. I just have to remind myself that it's relevant for them to know it, too."

"Okay, good. I think you've got a good conceptual approach. But take a couple of days to think about it further. Don't forget your normal work load, either. Figure out what help you'll need, like technical assistance, visuals—you'll probably need someone from IT. Remember your deadline; break it down into intermediate time frames for partial completion. Don't leave anything to chance." Ruth got up and moved toward the door, then looked back. "Oh, and I'd like for you to think about what you want to learn from doing this, too."

"I don't know whether to say thanks or not," Art told her.

Two days later, they met again, this time at Ruth's conference table, which contained only a small pad and a pencil until Art plunked down two notebooks and a couple of loose pages of notes.

"How's it been going?" Ruth began. "Have you had a chance to think about the presentation?"

"Yeah. I've put some real time in on it. I'm not sure I'm on the right track, though, because I've never had to do anything quite like this before."

"It's a pretty big challenge, but you have to do it right. I have a few questions that will let me know where your thinking is at this point."

"Okay."

Ruth ticked off a small item on her pad. "First question: what do you feel your basic targets should be on this?"

"Well, I think top management is going to be a lot more interested in costs and benefits, so that's one target. Another is to make a readable history of the project that details what we've done and how close we came to our original plans. And I'm sure I should have a couple of things I'll want to highlight."

"All right," Ruth responded. "Do you have some kind of a basic outline for the report?"

Art shuffled through his notes. "Yeah, kind of a skeleton, but . . here it is. First I summarize the history of the project—where it came from and where it hooks into the overall strategy. Then a statement of project goals—what our philosophy of service is, our strategy of analysis, the chronology of the analysis results, assessment, and cost-benefits analysis. And finally some conclusions and a summary of what we've learned for the future."

"I think you're basically on the right track. I've got some things I want to make sure are included, and you've hit most of them. But the most important thing to get across is the fact that you came in on time and under budget and actually improved and simplified the analytical process. That's got to come through at every opportunity."

"Got it," said Art, saluting and smiling.

"One more thing, then," said Ruth. "What's your learning goal for yourself?"

Art closed the lid on his laptop and sat back. He thought for a while, then said, "I've always been pretty organized and technically creative, but much more of a hands-on guy than a word guy. This presentation will force me to put everything together. The biggest thing, though, will be actually presenting and defending the report in front of umpteen people who drive Porsches."

Ruth asked, "What'll you do about that?"

"Well, I'll have to have a really good plan—one I can trust. And I'll have to know *you* like the plan and think it'll work. Then I'll have to have excellent visuals to support the show. Oh, and I think I'd like to have a sort of rehearsal. Maybe you could throw tough questions at me."

"You took the words right out of my mouth. I also want to be comfortable that you can hold up your end in the meeting. OK, what timeline do you have for making sure you meet the deadline and are well prepared?"

Art opened his laptop. "I probably won't have to do much research—I was in on the project from the beginning—and I've already been putting together my notes. I should be able to rough them out in a week or so, then give what I have to word processing. Then, after you've reviewed it,

I should be able to put the finishing touches to it in three or four days. Tomorrow morning I'm meeting with design and IT for the visuals—they'll have a firm deadline on those. Everything should come together three or four days before the presentation, so I'll have time to polish it and dry-run it with you."

"What do you need from me, then?" asked Ruth. "And when do you need it?"

"First, I want your overall view of the project's history and your sense of its relative success. If I can make it clear to an outsider, it should be pretty good."

"Then?"

"Then the review and the rehearsal. But I'm sure a lot of questions will pop up as I go along, so I'll probably bug you with them."

"Bug away. But do you think you might run into any problems or obstacles?"

"I'm not too worried about *my* assignments, but I'm not as confident in getting stuff from other people. I need some data from finance to compile the final cost-benefits statement, so there could be a snag there. And the audiovisual stuff. I may need to dog those people from day one."

"Now how are you going to monitor your progress?" Ruth asked. "Do you want any suggestions from me? This is an important project and I want to make sure we have an 'early warning system' for anything that might come up."

Making a Developmental Assignment

The best mentors are always looking for opportunities to help their mentees learn on the job. If you want to fit into this category you're going to have to carry your mentees around in your head; to have "mentee on the brain." One way to do this is to make a conscious effort to note real-life situations that you can use as teaching opportunities. By drawing your assignments from the things around you, you will be using mentoring as a strategic tool— one that challenges your partner to grow and stretch by trying new things on the job. Of course, if you're not the mentee's direct manager you are not empowered to make such assignments. No matter. You're still going to want to have discussions that are both probing and developmental concerning current projects your mentees are working on. You may also explore challenging projects that your mentee could work on with his or her manager's permission. A regular series of such meetings will allow you to mentor them throughout the project—from coaching in advance to reviewing progress once the project is completed.

This is *real-time* mentoring because it involves your mentees into a production and delivery situation in which they are expected to perform as well as learn. In this sense, the mentoring is going on while you are both doing something else. You are pursuing your other responsibilities; your partner is carrying out an assignment that is of value to the organization.

These kinds of projects come in all descriptions but they all allow the mentee to learn from performing them. However, these assignments must not be make-work projects; they must have intrinsic meaning and importance so that success or failure is more than just a learning experience. The fact that there is consequence connected to the outcome is as essential to the learning value as the experience of working on the assignment in the first place. A challenge is not a challenge if it is not a relevant task. The types of activities that most mentees find challenging and meaningful include small-scale start-up projects; well-defined fix-it or "rescue" plans; projects that will be seen by many people; and redesigns of existing processes.

Tactical mentoring and coaching play a crucial part in making the strategic project work. After the project is created, your primary mentoring job is to prepare your partners for the mission and to assist them in designing a plan of attack. Throughout the project you should be available for coaching, advice, and assistance whenever your mentees need it. When the project is finished, after-action mentoring is invaluable as a feedback and learning tool for your partners. Assisting them to systematically reflect on their success or failure and to consider alternatives for future action reinforces the assignment's value as a practical, real-life learning experience.

```
┌─────────────┐     ┌─────────────┐     ┌─────────────┐
│ Pre-Project │     │             │     │ After Action│
│  Tactical   │ ──▶ │Developmental│ ──▶ │  Tactical   │
│  Mentoring  │     │  Project    │     │  Mentoring  │
└─────────────┘     └─────────────┘     └─────────────┘
```

Projects that are strategic to an individual's development are usually new and untried experiences for the person. You will want to use questioning to help your mentees think through a plan of attack, but you're likely to have to give them some real suggestions and guidance, as well. You know how you would want the project performed, so you must be able to guide your mentees on methods of completing the job successfully. You may be aware of pitfalls you can warn them about, or of certain individuals to be wary of. Think about how you can balance your questioning with suggestions and advice.

A Few General Guidelines

Be clear about your expectations for the project. When the project is agreed to, you should be concerned about two things: the outcome of the project and the knowledge your mentee receives from it. Get as clear a picture as you possibly can on what you want the outcomes and the learning results to be. In other words, what do you and your mentee want the outcomes to look like when all is said and done? If you both possess the same mental picture of the desired results, you greatly enhance the likelihood of success.

Give your mentee an opportunity to contribute to the plan of execution. After you have painted your picture of outcomes, ask your mentees to think critically about how they should approach the project how they would prepare a plan of attack.

Listen to your mentee's thinking and approach to the project. This is the time to be a careful, probing listener. Hear your partners' ideas, but ask many questions. Help them develop a critical ear to the project that will make it easier for them to develop alternative approaches and arguments. This is your opportunity to apply your "internal checklist" for project planning and go through it with your partners.

Set clear goals—both project completion goals and learning goals— for your mentees. The quality of the goals you establish at this point will relate directly to the quality of the dialogue you have with your mentees on their plan of attack. The goals you set together should be as explicit as possible and contain an accurate, mutually endorsed picture of the outcomes you both want.

Teach your mentees what they need to know. By definition, developmental projects are first-time experiences. It is likely that your partner does not know how—or may not have the skills needed—to be totally successful on the project. Find out what the person needs and do the necessary teaching, training, and advising that will stack the project for success. People learn more from successes than failures. When your mentee has had success in a project, your after-action mentoring can build on strengths instead of correcting mistakes and improving weaknesses.

Always have a plan for monitoring progress. We've already identified two stages of mentoring that are essential for the mentee's learning and growth: mentoring prior to the work and mentoring as an after-action review. Just as important, though, is an agreed upon, well-planned process for tracking your mentee's progress during the project. You must determine together how you will monitor the course of the project and how you will identify and correct problems if it becomes necessary.

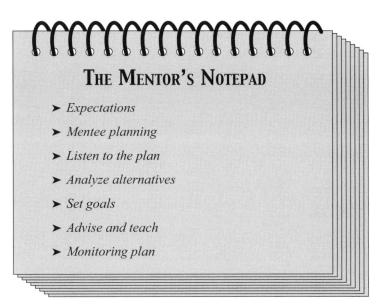

THE MENTOR'S NOTEPAD

➤ *Expectations*

➤ *Mentee planning*

➤ *Listen to the plan*

➤ *Analyze alternatives*

➤ *Set goals*

➤ *Advise and teach*

➤ *Monitoring plan*

CHECKLIST Nº 1

Here, Try This (for pre-project discussion)

✓ This is a project I want you to take on. This is what the result should look like.

✓ What do you feel your target should be on this project?

✓ What is your production goal?

- What time line should you have?

- What will it take to get it done within the proper time line?

- What do you need to get started?

- What past project experience will help you in working on this?

✓ Who do you need with you on this?

✓ Who do you need to coordinate with?

✓ What preparation should you be doing?

✓ How long will it take you to complete your preparation?

✓ What resources should you gather before beginning?

✓ What external resources will you need?

✓ What internal resources will you need?

✓ What is your plan of attack?

✓ What is your learning goal?

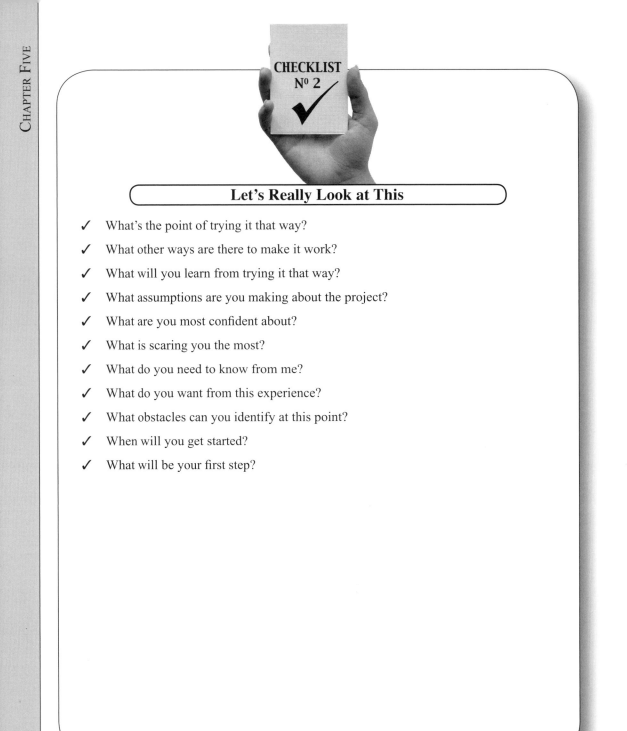

CHECKLIST Nº 2

Let's Really Look at This

✓ What's the point of trying it that way?

✓ What other ways are there to make it work?

✓ What will you learn from trying it that way?

✓ What assumptions are you making about the project?

✓ What are you most confident about?

✓ What is scaring you the most?

✓ What do you need to know from me?

✓ What do you want from this experience?

✓ What obstacles can you identify at this point?

✓ When will you get started?

✓ What will be your first step?

CHECKLIST Nº 3

Refining the Plan

✓ What efficiencies do you have to try to achieve as you develop the project?

✓ How will you monitor your progress?

✓ How should I be involved in the monitoring process?

✓ How will you know when you need help?

✓ How often should we communicate during the project?

✓ I need an "early warning system. "How will you notify me of problems arising?

✓ What challenges do you foresee to your "way of thinking" in performing this activity?

✓ How will this assignment challenge you to alter your way of thinking about projects?

✓ How will you flag your need to think "out of the box" as the project proceeds?

✓ What will happen if you do it the way you plan?

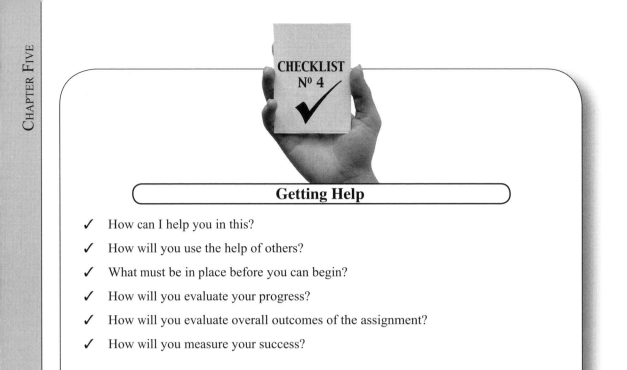

Getting Help

✓ How can I help you in this?

✓ How will you use the help of others?

✓ What must be in place before you can begin?

✓ How will you evaluate your progress?

✓ How will you evaluate overall outcomes of the assignment?

✓ How will you measure your success?

**CHECKLIST
Nº 5**

✔

This Is What I Want You to Accomplish

✓ This is my suggestion for what might work best.

✓ Watch out for this pitfall: _____.

✓ This pitfall has caused this in the past: _____.

✓ When you're finished with this step, come back and tell me what you've learned about _____.

✓ Be careful with him (her).

✓ If you need me to intervene with _____, let me know; but I'll want an analysis of why and how.

✓ Tell me what part of my suggestion you think might not work.

✓ If you take the tack you're suggesting, it'll probably have this effect: _____.

✓ Let's brainstorm how to do that; I've got some ideas.

✓ This is the reason I want you to work on this:_____.

✓ This is what I think you'll gain from working on this: _____.

✓ This is what success on this will do for us: _____.

✓ These are the prices for failing on this: _____.

CHAPTER 6

Learning from a Developmental Assignment

"There is a great person who makes everyone feel small. But the really great person is the one who makes everyone feel great.

—CHINESE PROVERB

SCENARIO 5

Ruth and Art

The report and presentation on the original emplacement project was completed on the 3rd of the month. The entire top management team was present as Art delivered the main part of the report. While Art had done quite a good job on the project itself, Ruth felt that the presentation itself lacked the open, integrative quality she thought it should have. All the data was there, and the program was well-planned, but Art's need for more practice and confidence in such things was evident. The management group was not disappointed; in fact, the report was pretty well received, but Ruth wants to make sure that Art gets in touch with the things he needs to work on.

Art suggested that they meet in Ruth's office, as his was too littered with books, notes, and graphs to be presentable. He has gathered up some of these items—the actual outline and presentation materials he used in the show—and brought them with him to the meeting.

"Let's sit down over here so we can spread this stuff out," Ruth began, pointing to the round conference table, which had been recently polished to a fine finish. "What I'd like to do is review how the presentation went—what worked, what didn't, what you learned."

"I'm just relieved that it's over," Art said as he sat down. "What a chore!"

Ruth sat across from him and asked, "In your opinion, what went best? What are you proudest of?"

"Well, we met our goal: we summarized the project thoroughly and intelligently and got our results across. I'll admit that the project kind of spoke for itself because of how well it went off. But I think the presentation was organized and the visuals worked well. I'm kind of proud of the planning and preparing I did."

"Yes, you worked up a strong approach and followed your plan."

"And I don't think any of the executives walked out of there with any unanswered questions. We made sure to let them know that we came in on time and under budget. And better yet, the customer was pleased."

"I agree. The data you presented was very clear. I felt good not only about your presentation of the information, but your run-up to the delivery date. You hit your targets all along the way. You were always ready to proceed to the next step. I also liked the way we worked together and how you worked with Janine. She was happy about that, too. Now, what, if anything, didn't go as well as it should have from your point of view? What would you do differently if you could do it over again?"

"I don't know. I feel good about all of

it. I got through it. I was scared, but I'm still alive. I don't mean to be superficial, but I'm more satisfied than I expected to be. What do you think?"

Ruth looked right at Art. "I think you're too happy to have it over with."

"Uh. What do you mean?"

"I mean that I think there is some room for improvement in the *style and manner* with which you put the report over. I'm not saying that the fact that you were nervous was a problem. What I saw was that you seemed convinced that as long as your data were correct and presented in a logical way, that was enough. And don't get me wrong, that *is* extremely important. It's just not sufficient when reporting to top management, that's all. We worked on that in our practice sessions, but I think you got up there and kind of forgot about it."

"Fill me in, I'm not getting you yet."

"Okay. For example, you didn't provide really adequate

opportunity for questions early on. That was probably a result of your nervousness and will work itself out with practice. But what I want you to be aware of here is that you seemed to feel that the very fact that someone asked a question meant that you hadn't covered what you should have and that there was something wrong. Did you feel that way?"

"Gee, I don't recall… I guess I wished I didn't have to be questioned, that I had been clear enough in the first place."

"That's what I'm talking about. When you got questions that interrupted your planned talk, you would get just a little defensive, not a lot, but a little. Do you remember feeling any of that?"

Art, frowning, admitted, "Yeah, I think I'm afraid I'll get pushed off my plan and lose my train of thought. I just wish I could get through the thing before I "flame out" so to speak."

"Do you think they are challenging you when they ask questions?"

"Well, aren't they sometimes?"

"I suppose at times that can be a motivation some might have, but I'm convinced that most of the time people ask questions because they just 'have a question.' I don't think most people do it to show you up. As a matter of fact, it's been my experience that your audience usually wants you to succeed, because if you succeed, they end up hearing an interesting, informative presentation."

"Uh huh."

Then Ruth offered, "I want you to know that we're talking about fine-tuning here. I think you did a good job that a little polish will greatly improve. Tell me, what did you learn from making the presentation?"

"Well, I guess the main goal shouldn't be to just get through the thing alive. I think that's what it came to for me. Also, that every question doesn't mean disapproval."

"Yes."

"I'm thinking about it now. I think I'd like more practice—a lot more—and get you or whoever is working with me to really push back at me in rehearsal. Try to anticipate as many questions as possible. And work on relaxing and going with the needs of the people I'm talking to."

"But is it a good idea to try to anticipate every question?"

"It's my nature, but I can see that if I do, I might get panicked by getting a question I don't foresee. So I have to try to develop as much confidence as possible that I'll probably be able to deal with questions as they come."

"Here's something important to consider. Did anyone in the meeting ask you a question you didn't know the answer to?"

"No. I really don't see how they could have."

"Exactly. You were the foremost expert on the emplacement project. You knew all the answers because you designed the system and solved all the problems. Instead of feeling like a prisoner under a bright light, remind yourself that you know more about your subject than anyone in the company."

"I like that," Art replied. "If I forget, remind me."

"All right. Can you think of any other way I can help?"

"You helped me in preparing the show and you're helping now. I'd say, let's just keep on this kind of track. I'd like to be able to ask you to rehearse me in the future and be rougher on me than the audience is likely to be."

Ruth concluded, "Practice and prepare yourself enough so that you feel relaxed. Resist getting into a formal presentation mode. Remember what I said about your expertise and you'll realize that your delivery is actually interactive, not just a performance."

After the Project Is Over

It's easy to forget about tactical mentoring once an activity has been completed. There is a great temptation to breathe a sigh of relief, hand out compliments, and get on to the next challenge. If you're like most people you feel that there is much to do and little time to do it. And reviewing a completed mission—especially a successful one—feels like wasting time. But after-action mentoring is not only a good idea; the learning your mentees will get from it is often richer than what they get from conventional pre-project mentoring. It gives you both the opportunity to review the project's history and discuss the actual experience the mentee has had. You can compare performance goals and actual performance. Your mentees can evaluate their experience compared to the learning goals you agreed on before the task was begun. You can share your evaluation of their performance and give them feedback based on the project outcomes as well as on your mentees' behavior, comprehension, improvement, and thinking process.

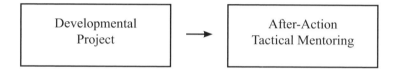

Use the opportunity to take stock of alternatives that can be applied to future experiences. After-action mentoring allows you and your mentees to

★ consolidate what they have learned from their experience in working on the assignment
★ correct any mistakes and learn from them
★ develop new lessons and alternatives for the future
★ examine their thinking process and consider how it serves or hinders
★ learn about their behavior patterns, habits, talents, and opportunities for growth
★ apply what they have learned to specific new projects

A Few General Guidelines

Ask your mentees to share what they think went well and not so well in the undertaking. The review should be a learning experience for both of you; you have a definite opinion of how the project came off, but your partners may have a different interpretation.

Share your honest impressions and assessment with your mentees. This is the time to be completely clear and descriptive about what you are most and least satisfied with in your mentees' performance. Your honest feedback at this time can be very instructive. By giving specific feedback and by describing the

effect their performance has had, you are really telling them what you are truly looking for and what your real standards are.

Analyze alternatives your mentees might use next time out. Always take a teaching attitude into the review. Use everything that comes up in the discussion as a teaching and coaching opportunity. Have your mentees model the behavior you want to encourage in them. For instance, if you want to teach them to become more adept at self-assessment, ask them to assess their own performance on the project. If you want to teach self-management, ask them what they will do differently as a result of this project experience.

Ask how you can be of help. Remember that you've thrust your mentees out of their comfort zone and into a possibly stressful experience. Understand and respect this discomfort. The experience you and your mentees have in working on developmental activities teaches you both valuable lessons about how to make future experiments fruitful. Your mentees will have very useful suggestions on how you can aid them in their next endeavors.

Rely on these easy-to-remember guidelines. Ask your mentee
- what went well?
- what didn't go so well?
- what have you learned from the experience?
- how can I help?

Mixing Feedback

Do not only ask questions. Share your impressions and assessments. It's important that your mentees deal with their own conclusions about the experience, but they need to hear your frank impressions, too. Whether it's corrective or confirming of good performance, or whether it is sharing your take on how the mentees handled themselves with others, your opinion is crucially important in their understanding of what they have done and what remains to be worked on. Your challenge is to mix your own feedback effectively with the self-feedback you draw out from your mentees.

THE MENTOR'S NOTEPAD

➤ *What went well?*

➤ *What didn't?*

➤ *Give some specific praise or corrections.*

➤ *Tell the effects.*

➤ *What have you learned?*

➤ *How can I help?*

How Did It Go?

✓ How would you evaluate your experience on this assignment? From the point of view of outcomes? From the point of view of value-added learning?

✓ How would you rate yourself and your performance on this?

✓ What have you accomplished?

✓ Did you experience any conflicts with others while on the project? If so, what action did you take to effectively manage the conflict?

✓ What major problems did you experience?

✓ How did you overcome them?

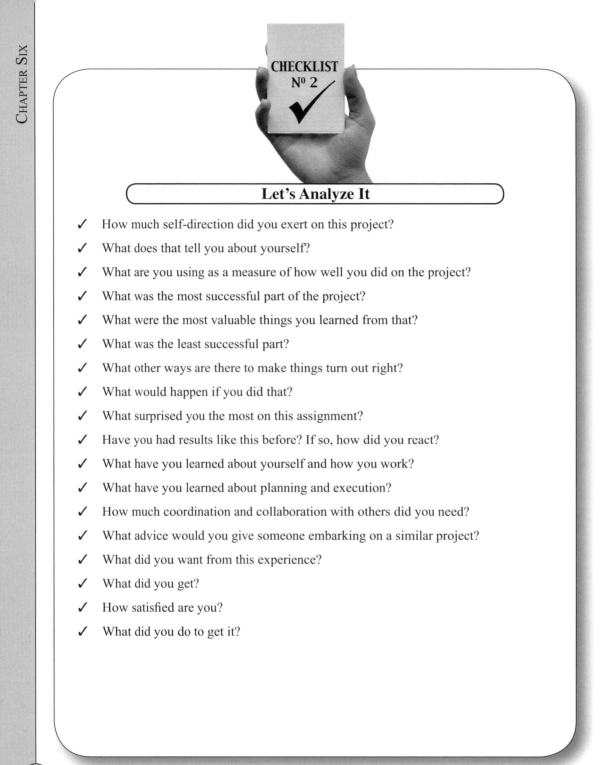

CHECKLIST Nº 2

Let's Analyze It

✓ How much self-direction did you exert on this project?

✓ What does that tell you about yourself?

✓ What are you using as a measure of how well you did on the project?

✓ What was the most successful part of the project?

✓ What were the most valuable things you learned from that?

✓ What was the least successful part?

✓ What other ways are there to make things turn out right?

✓ What would happen if you did that?

✓ What surprised you the most on this assignment?

✓ Have you had results like this before? If so, how did you react?

✓ What have you learned about yourself and how you work?

✓ What have you learned about planning and execution?

✓ How much coordination and collaboration with others did you need?

✓ What advice would you give someone embarking on a similar project?

✓ What did you want from this experience?

✓ What did you get?

✓ How satisfied are you?

✓ What did you do to get it?

CHECKLIST
Nº 3

✓

How About Next Time?

✓ What would you make sure to repeat next time?

✓ What different directions would have produced more efficiency?

✓ Did you ever have to go to plan B?

✓ How well did you manage your time on the project?

✓ How well did you manage your resources throughout the assignment?

✓ When, if ever, did you feel a loss of control over what was happening?

✓ If so, what action did you take?

✓ What action do you wish you would have taken?

✓ What did you learn on this project that will help you on the next one?

✓ What skills should you have mastered before beginning the project?

✓ What preparations will you make sure of next time?

✓ What processes did you use in making decisions on this assignment?

✓ Would you repeat the process? Why?

✓ What did you get from me that helped most? Least?

✓ How would you handle that in the future?

**CHECKLIST
Nº 4**

This Is What I See

✓ This is my overall evaluation of the outcome.

✓ This is what my highest expectation was.

✓ This is what is tolerable to have achieved.

✓ This is how happy/unhappy I am with the result.

✓ This is what I've seen you do on it.

✓ This is what I've seen you learn on it.

✓ This is what I've seen you improve in.

✓ This is what I see you still needing to work on.

✓ This is how I feel it would have worked if you had done _____.

✓ This is how others should have reacted to the outcome.

✓ This is what I was after.

✓ What alternative plans could get you to that outcome?

✓ What is most important in making it come out as we need it?

Epilogue

The primary message of this book has been that the mentor is the vehicle by which the mentee learns, grows, and discovers. The goal of every mentor must be to act in such a way with your mentees that they become more able to do for themselves. By accepting the designation "mentor," you take on the charge to empower your mentees *to think, to embrace responsibility, to take increased risks for growth, and to increase their very capacity.*

The second most important message is that we must not give in to the temptation to think of "helping" as "doing for." Mentoring is one person's attempt to help another to do for him or herself. This begins when the mentor strategically affects the professional life of the mentee by fostering insight, identifying needed knowledge, and expanding the mentee's horizons.

For this to happen successfully, the relationship between mentor and mentee must flow with openness and trust. It must be an exquisitely *adult partnership*, with each person taking responsibility and acting authentically with the other. A mature mentoring partnership demonstrates an ongoing fascination with learning and discovery and an open dialogue between the partners. It is essential that you learn your mentees' needs. If they don't fully trust you, they won't open up to you. Only if the trust is implicit and complete can mentoring focus on and address the issues that will be of greatest benefit to the mentees.

Here are six important keys to the mentoring dialogue. If you remember and strive to practice them face to face, a full-grown partnership should result—a partnership characterized by mutual investment, flexibility to respond to current needs and learning situations and shared growth.

1. *The mentee and I both win if our best thinking emerges and the mentee owns and is committed to action.* My role is not to control, take over, or simply provide answers.

2. *Our purpose is to go beyond what either of us knows or can contribute as an individual.* Mentoring is a partnership in which both parties learn.

3. *I will examine my own thinking and ideas before advocating a course action to my mentee.* I will encourage the mentee to find the

weakness or incompleteness in my thinking. The mentee will grow, and I will learn.

4. *I will delve into my own motives for taking a position on an issue with my mentee.* I will bring my biases and assumptions to the surface and keep them where I and my mentee can keep an eye on them.

5. *We will sustain a spirit in our relationship that allows us to share our suggestions and ideas.* We will also be able to share our "ways of thinking" from whence the suggestions and ideas spring.

6. *I will view my mentee as a colleague.* I will value the worthiness of the idea over the rank of the person expressing it.

Other Mentoring Products
By
Perrone-Ambrose Associates

A MENTOR'S COMPANION by Larry Ambrose, offers a journey through the mentoring interaction. It combines live dialogues between a VP, Ruth, and her mentee, Art, with behavior menus and action steps.

THE MENTORING FIELD GUIDE by Perrone-Ambrose Associates, Inc., collects the action checklists from A Mentor's Companion and presents them in an easy-to-find-and-use format. It will simplify preparation for mentoring sessions.

THE MENTEE'S NAVIGATOR by Jim Perrone & Larry Ambrose. This workbook-handbook is for those who want to take charge of their careers. It presents principles for mentee success; allows mentees to track their progress and chronicle lessons learned.

COMMON SENSE MENTORING by Larry Ambrose talks sense to both mentors and mentees about the "little" questions, those bugaboos and puzzlers they will likely experience, which are often more important than the grand mentoring principles.

MENTOR'S BOOKMARK A 3" X 8" laminate that states the practices of a highly effective mentor.

MENTEE'S BOOKMARK A 3" X 8" laminate that states the five declarations of a skilled mentee.

MENTOR'S 2100 SKILLS AUDIT A 360° feedback tool that measures 6 critical skills for a mentor, coach, facilitator and/or manager and scores input from self, supervisor and up to 10 direct reports

MENTORING & COACHING POCKET PROMPTER A triple-fold pocket card that lists competencies, questions, hints and reminders for the mentor.

COMPASS FOR MENTORING & COACHING A 6" x 8" card that displays a framework for conducting the mentoring session. The reverse side lists 32 questions to be used by the mentor/coach in the sessions.

MENTOR SELF ASSESSMENT Allows mentors to assess their mentoring skills, behaviors and opinions; for use as a part of mentor skills training or as a stand-alone. (Initial minimum order of five.)

MENTEE SELF ASSESSMENT Employees can rate themselves on behaviors associated with successful mentees: receptivity, self-management, self-awareness, growth orientation, resilience and double-loop learning focus. This information can be shared and discussed with mentors/coaches if desired. (Initial minimum order of five.)

www.perrone-ambrose.com

Notes

Notes

Notes

Notes